As We See . . .

Aboriginal
Pedagogy

EDITED BY
LENORE A. STIFFARM

Printed in Canada by Hignell Printing, Winnipeg, Manitoba

The excerpt on pages 2–3 is reprinted with the permission of Scribner, a Division of Simon & Schuster from *The Same River Twice* by Alice Walker, Copyright © 1996 by Alice Walker.

The excerpt on page 29 is reprinted with permission from *Earth Elder Stories.* Copyright 1988 by Alexander Wolfe (Calgary: Fifth House Ltd.).

The excerpt on page 32 is reprinted with permission from *Keepers of the Animals.* Copyright 1991 by M. Caduto and J. Bruchac (Calgary: Fifth House Ltd.).

The excerpt on page 61 is reprinted from *Black Elk Speaks*, by John G. Neihardt, by permission of the University of Nebraska Press. Copyright 1932, 1959, 1972, by John G. Neihardt Trust.

The excerpt from Sterling on page 109 is reprinted with permission of the Publisher from Marie Battiste and Jean Barman, eds., *First Nations Education in Canada: The Circle Unfolds* (Vancouver: The University of British Columbia Press, 1995). All rights reserved by the Publisher.

Quotations of more than three lines in this publication have been printed with the permissions of the copyright holders or their designates.

Canadian Cataloguing in Publication Data

Main entry under title:

As we see— : aboriginal pedagogy

Includes bibliographical references.
ISBN 0-88880-384-2

1. Native peoples—Education—Canada.* 2. Native peoples—Canada—Social life and customs.* 3. Native peoples—Canada—Rites and ceremonies.* I. Stiffarm, Lenore A.

E96.2.A79 1998   305.897'071   C98-920182-1

DEDICATION

To all of my teachers—elders George Goodstriker, Joe Ironman, John
Allen, Jr., John Mark Stiffarm, Gordon Belcourt; the late John
Moosiman, lodge keeper; and to my children—They-Wus, White Moon,
Medicine Eagle—and to grandchildren Holy Singing Eagle Woman,
Rock Boy and Brandon.

University Extension Press

University of Saskatchewan

Dean of the Extension Division: Gordon Thompson
Managing Editor of the Press: Bertram Wolfe
Copy editing and layout: Clare Fairbairn
Proofreading: Allison Muri

CONTENTS

PREFACE

LENORE A. STIFFARM

The art work for the cover of this book has been developed by my
son, a young Ah Ah Ni Nin (White Clay) artist, "Medicine Eagle,"
a.k.a. A. J. Stiffarm, age 15, grade 10 at Harlem High School, Harlem,
Montana. He is a grass dancer, plays basketball, runs cross country and
beads in his spare time. This is the first art work that he created, and
shows the Aboriginal woman who, according to White Clay tradition, is
the keeper of knowledge as well as the transmitter of knowledge. It is
called "As She Sees . . ."; this book, then, is an extension of "As She
Sees . . ."

> *As We See . . . Aboriginal Pedagogy* is a way for Aboriginal people
> to give voice,
> to give dignity,
> to give respect,
> to give courage

to all of the Grandfathers and Grandmothers and their relatives who
have given us the strength to continue on.

"First Nations" is a term used by many people in Canada to
designate the Aboriginal people. "First" denotes primacy "Nation"
indicates that the people were organized into social, political and
economic groups with distinct cultures and languages and lands; and the
plural form notes diversity of these groups. This term was a result of
the National Indian Brotherhood, which has been renamed the
Assembly of First Nations. Throughout this text, First Nations, First
Peoples, Indians, Natives and Aboriginal People are also used
interchangeably to describe the indigenous peoples of North America.

ACKNOWLEDGEMENTS

When one undertakes the challenge of developing a book of this magnitude, it is shaped by many people and many forces. This book is no exception!

A very special acknowledgement goes to Bert Wolfe, Managing Editor of the University of Saskatchewan Extension Press; to Clare Fairbairn, for the copy editing and lay-out, as well as for the brochure he developed in advertising this book. A special thank-you goes to Gordon Thompson, Dean of the Extension Division of the University of Saskatchewan, for his commitment to this project. Priscilla Settee, Co-ordinator of the Aboriginal Program, Extension Divison, deserves a very sincere thank-you for her program's support. Dr. Michael Owen, Director of Research Services, University of Saskatchwan, deserves special recognition for his department generously providing me with a publications grant to assist with copy editing costs.

Thanks also go to A. J. Stiffarm for serving Migipneot, our Creator, with your creation of "As She Sees . . ." — keep up the excellent artistic creations. To the contributors of this collection, thank you because you have served as my teachers in this journey:

- Willie Ermine for your wisdom and inspiration throughout our class at Prince Albert. You never failed to inspire each of us on those early Saturday morning classes.
- Bente Huntley for your creativity and passion in how you believe in our elders. You have shown me how to walk with dignity.
- Ida Swan for your perseverance and "warrior ways" in all that you do in your role in education. You gave me the reason to continue on when I saw only darkness.
- Angelina Weenie for your gentleness in how you believe in the sacred circle of life. You continued to show us how all is connected.
- Jane Harp for your belief in our future leaders, those children of today. You helped me to walk my talk by you walking your talk.
- Wally Isbister for your "feistiness" in terms of how you learn most— through challenging and raising questions until you understand. You have taught me what perseverance means.

- Lillian Dyck for your dignity, perseverance, respect and belief in all of life. You have been an important teacher in my life by showing me what dignity, perseverance, respect and belief mean in the academic community.
- MaryAnne Lanigan for your vibrancy with story telling as a way of teaching. You have shown me the dedication and commitment it takes to teach through storytelling.
- to my family — They-Wus, White Moon, Medicine Eagle, and Little Bull — thank you for believing in me so that I might carry on.

Introduction

Lenore A. Stiffarm

For the past century or more, traditional knowledge was condemned as "heathen" or "folklore," but Aboriginal peoples' traditional teachings and knowledge are, at long last, being recognized as valid and valued. It is the resilience of Aborginal peoples, the world over, that has kept alive their oral traditions and teachings. [Huntley, "Plants and Medicines," this volume]

For many years, Aboriginal knowledge was invalidated by Western ways of knowing. This unconscious, subconscious and conscious means of invalidating Aboriginal knowledge served to perpetrate a superior/ inferior relationship around knowledge and how this knowledge is passed on. Systemic racism was clearly perpetrated in this way.

In recent times, there has been a plethora of interest and desire to know Aborginal ways of knowing and being. Many people have found that their ways were not working, nor were their ways fulfilling their lives.

As this collection of works shows, Aborginal people have had ways of teaching, ways of being and ways of knowing that have sustained us for the last 500 or more years. These ways were passed on just as they had been in the past. In some communities, due to the breakdown as a result of residential schools, reserves and European contact, many of these ways were quietly passed on. In some cases, severe punishment was used so that Aboriginal people would not continue on with ways that worked since time immemorial. Today, we Aboriginal people find ourselves at a place where many of us are ready to take on the challenge of giving voice to the richness that has been so close to us that we often do not consider these ways as special since they are so much of our daily life.

My paper, "Spirit Writing: Writing Circles as Healing Pedagogy," demonstrates how writing from one's spirit, one's soul, allows us to heal from traumas we experienced in our lives. I examine how we often become "stuck" in our inability to feel our feelings. Being stuck prevents us from living life to the fullest. It prevents us from fully enjoying our environment, our children, our families, our communities. In this article, I describe a process whereby Aboriginal people are letting go of the trauma in their lives in a safe, non-threatening way. Aborginal people have often not been able to say good-bye to loved ones, have not been able to give voice to what is "stuck" inside of us. Through spirit writing, Aborginal people are able to let go of these feelings so that we can claim our rightful place in today's society. These experiences have been used with groups from grade 1 through elders. Each has responded in an extremely positive way.

Willie Ermine's "Pedagogy from the Ethos: An Interview with Elder Ermine on Language" examines, through interview and dialogue, who is responsible for passing on the language and the "ethos" of the Cree speakers. Ermine eloquently refers to the "Older Ones" as being the keepers and transmitters of knowledge. Ermine stresses the importance of role "modelling" as a critical way of teaching. Ermine further points out the importance and central element of "protocol" as a means to access anything from the Elders. He clearly delineates the Aboriginal pedagogy for the ethos of Cree world-view and ends with "the basis for formation of an Aboriginal pedagogy in broader areas of language and culture."

Bente Huntley's "Plants and Medicines: An Aboriginal Way of Teaching" explores, through interviews with elders as well as an extensive review of the literature, how to develop curriculum for Saskatchewan Aboriginal learners. Huntley's expertise as an instructor strengthens her work since she has first-hand knowledge of how to "clear the regulation barriers" with Saskatchewan Education. However, she is most respectful in providing a clear voice and accurate traditional environmental knowledge of the elders' appropriate perspective. It is with this foundation that she sets out to succinctly demonstrate the importance of passing on critical Aboriginal pedagogy to future generations. Her work unfolds naturally while she weaves tradition with respect.

Ida Swan's "Modelling: An Aboriginal Approach" explores the clashes between Western and Aboriginal educational ideology. Swan points out very clearly how, for example, the provincial guidelines for education, with which locals bands are bound, clash with the local Aboriginal art of teaching. For high school completions to be recognized, bands are forced to comply with the provincial guidelines. These guidelines take young people out of the environment for learning at the same time when traditional ways of knowing are to be passed on. Swan uses the Northern Cree ways of knowing as the foundation for her arguments.

Angelina Weenie's "Aboriginal Pedagogy: The Sacred Circle Concept" offers glimpses of the medicine wheel as a foundation for teaching. She explores Indigenous ways of knowing as the foundation for showing interconnectedness, relationships and a holistic way of presenting the art of teaching. She draws upon the works of Robert Regnier as well as Richard Katz and Verna St. Denis as a way of setting the context. She ends with the eloquent philosophy set forth by Black Elk.

Jane Harp's "Traditional Parenting" is similar to Ida Swan's work in that both draw on the strength of traditional Indian values as a foundation for Aboriginal pedagogy. However, Harp explores her work in the context of traditional parenting as the foundation for making this change. She draws upon the Cree and Ojibway ways of knowing as the foundation for illustrating the traditional concepts she proposes. Her stories show how traditional parenting was sustained, and provide an excellent mirror even for today's parenting.

Wally Isbister's "A Piece of the Pie: The Inclusion of Aboriginal Pedagogy into the Structures of Public Education" provides a paradoxical but comprehensive journey into how Wally Isbister, as a Cree educator, has come to terms with the structures of public education as a foundation for the inclusion of Aboriginal pedagogy. He is passionate about his beliefs as a Cree educator in exploring "A Piece of the Pie."

Lillian Dyck's "An Analysis of Western Science Using the Medicine Wheel of the Plains Indians" draws on Indigenous knowledge as a way of making sense of Western linear reductionist paradigms. She provides illustrations of the contradictions of Western science. She also provides a glimpse of feminist scientific analysis. Then she moves into providing her interpretation of Western linear reductionist methods, drawing on the medicine wheel as a way of providing a foundation for this interpretation. Towards the end of her article, she points out how she has inverted the potentialities of the east and west directions. However, she explains how she enters the circle and her background of growing up outside of her Cree culture as the way she makes sense of her reality. She provides a medicine wheel that shows the way in which Cree people use it.

MaryAnne Lanigan's "Aboriginal Pedagogy: Storytelling" explores the importance of storytelling as the "oldest of the arts in every culture." Morrison examines myth and narrative as critical foundations of storytelling, showing how each has an important part of the circle. She provides examples of how effective storytelling can be with all children. She also provides an example of the story of "Wesakaychak and Wetiko." In her summary, she calls for a reintroduction and revalidation of storytelling, since all cultures have stories to share.

Spirit Writing: Writing Circles as Healing Pedagogy

Lenore A. Stiffarm

"I've never been given permission to say good-bye to my brother, sister, mother, father." These are the words echoed by many Aboriginal people as they began their healing journey.

Several years ago, I had the honour of going to see *Schindler's List*—what a powerful story of the Jewish journey. As I reflected upon the movie, it occurred to me that Aboriginal people have not even begun to tell our story.

We have a story to tell. Our story is beautiful, but tragic. It is filled with richness.

It is filled with pain.

It is filled with humiliation.

It is filled with vibrancy.

It is filled with shame.

It is filled with resiliency.

It is filled with grief.

It is filled with hope.

There are many ways to heal. We heal through individual counselling, group therapy and use of tranquillizers, anti-depressants or painkillers. We use court systems and the clergy to help us heal.

We also heal by yawning, sleeping, exercising, journaling, writing and talking. Through "spirit writing" and "spirit talking," Aboriginal people are giving voice to this pain. In writing circles, Aboriginal people do not have to worry about dotting the *i*'s and crossing the *t*'s.

So often, Aboriginal people have been made to feel ashamed of their feelings. They have been criticized, taunted and shamed for feeling sad about their losses. Through residential school trauma, Aboriginal people have stifled their pain. This is evident in the exorbitant alcoholism rate among our people. It is evident in the astronomical suicide rate within our

1

communities. It is evident in rampant domestic violence, sexual abuse and incest, and the obesity and relationship addictions we face. Through these various outlets, Aboriginal people are expressing these traumas.

Writing circles have been a way in which Aboriginal people can come together to explore their trauma in a safe, non-threatening environment. Many proponents of natural processes do not subscribe to this way of healing, which they consider "unnatural." For example, Wilson Schaef subscribes to the theory of allowing one to feel the feelings as they come about, not to intervene with these feelings by using drugs, anti-depressants or painkillers. On the other hand, some theorists feel that one should not be allowed to feel the feelings, and quickly prescribe tranquillizers to stop the feelings of sadness, pain or loss. Writing circles are used as a way for some of us who become "stuck" in our feelings. For example, many Aboriginal people have "frozen" their feelings because of the trauma experienced in residential school, whether it be sexual abuse, physical, mental, spiritual, emotional abuse, abandonment, cultural losses, losses of relationships, losses through death or losses through foster care placement. Alice Walker eloquently writes about this journey in *The Same River Twice*:

> I belong to a people so wounded by betrayal, so hurt by misplacing their trust, that to offer us a gift of love is often to risk one's life, certainly one's name and reputation. I do not mean only the Africans, sold and bought, and bought and sold again; or the Indians, who joyfully fed those who, when strong, gleefully starved them out. I speak as well of the shadowy European ancestor, resentfully denied, except that one cannot forget the thatched one-room hovels of old Europe, put to the torch by those who grabbed the land; and the grief of the starving, ashen ancestor, forced to seek his or her lonely fortune in a land that seemed to demand ruthlessness if one intended to survive.
>
> I belong to a people, heart and mind, who do not trust mirrors. Not those, in any case, in which we ourselves appear. The empty mirror, the one that reflects noses and hair unlike our own, and a prosperity and harmony we may never have known, gives us peace. Our shame is deep, for shame is the result of soul injury. Mirrors, however, are sacred, not only because they permit us to witness the

body we are fortunate this time around to be in, but because they permit us to ascertain the condition of the eternal that rests behind the body, the soul. [Walker, 1996, preface]

Gregory Cajete uses writing as a primary means of reaching our feelings:

Tribal teaching and learning were intertwined with the daily lives of both teacher and learner. . . . [T]he cultivation of one's senses through learning how to listen, observe and experience . . . was highly valued. . . . [T]he ability to use language through story telling, oratory, and song was highly regarded . . . as a primary tool for teaching and learning. This was because the spoken or sung word expressed the spirit and breath of life of the speaker, and thus was considered sacred. [Cajete, 1994, p. 33]

Cajete provides a glimpse of what happens with writing circles when he talks about "the expressed . . . spirit and breath of life."

THE CONTEXT

Often, Aboriginal people have no name for the feelings that they are feeling. As a way of setting the context, when these sessions occur, each person is provided an explanation that smudge will be used (see glossary at end of book for a note on smudge). Participants are given a choice as to whether they would like to smudge. In this way, our culture is used to connect the ceremony with the process of healing. Each session is started by reiterating that we are in ceremony. When we are in ceremony, we call upon all of those spirit helpers to sit with us and to help us through the process. Participants are then taken through a gentle, relaxing exercise by slowing stretching, breathing and preparing for a deep meditation. They are gently walked through the experience of relaxing their facial muscles, neck, shoulders, midriff, stomach and buttocks; of stretching their hamstrings and quadriceps. Affirmations are offered throughout this stretching exercise. Each person is told to hug herself or himself. Each person is told to say, "I am so beautiful." "I am so wonderful." "I am so intelligent." As these affirmations are completed, each person is asked to practise saying these affirmations on a daily basis. Immediately following this stretching exercise, the lights are lowered and each person is asked to find a comfortable place. This can be lying on the floor, sitting on a chair, curling in a ball—wherever one feels the most comfortable. Each person is given a sheet of paper and pencil. Meditation music is played very softly. Once everyone is settled, they are asked to take a couple of deep breaths in and to gently exhale. They are asked to shut their eyes and go to a safe place. This safe place could be whatever comes to mind. They are asked to mentally relax their toes, balls of their feet, heels, calves, knees, thighs, hips, pelvis. As they mentally move through the pelvis, they are asked to be aware of any pain they hold, especially those who have been sexually abused, violated, raped or fondled. Gently, moving on into the rib cage area, participants are asked to be aware of any tension they may be holding, to be aware of the breathing; to gently relax.

Moving into the heart area, participants are asked to mentally look into the heart area and be aware of any hurts they may be holding there. Is there a loved one who has passed on, and to whom you have not said good-bye? Perhaps you have lost your mother, father, brother, sister, uncle, aunt or grandparent and you were never able to say what you wanted to say. This is a time to take a look at those hurts, and as you are ready, gently release them. Have you felt abandoned in your life? Have you felt alone? This is the time to mentally examine what is in your heart. This is a safe place to be. And, as you are ready, to gently release.

Some of us have come from very violent homes. We have been mentally, physically, emotionally and spiritually abused. This is a time for us to mentally examine any hurts that we carry in our hearts, and, as we are ready, to gently release. Some of us have been placed in foster care and have grown up with many questions of "Why me?" As we explore these feelings, and as we are ready, we mentally release those feelings. Some of us have been abandoned through going to residential schools. Living in these institutions, we lost the community closeness and missed out on important ceremonies and the passing on of certain ways. This is a time for us to examine those losses, and as we are ready, to mentally release.

Some of us have experienced racism and have not known how to respond to the hurt and the pain of words in which we have "no breath of life" with which to respond. As a result, we have stifled those feelings. Some of us have had our children taken away from us and there has been an emptiness in our hearts. This is a time to take a look at that emptiness; to make peace with that emptiness. And, as we are ready, to mentally relax and release any feelings that we may be holding.

Let us move into our shoulder area. Be aware of any tension you might be holding in this area. Relax. Move into your upper arm area, elbow, wrists, fingers, thumbs. Gently relax. Move into your throat area. Some of us hold our pain in our throat area when we are holding in our tears. Be aware of any pain you may be holding in this area and, as you are ready, gently release. Mentally move into your mouth area. This is a time to be aware of any words we may have said that we would like to release. Often, we may have said hurtful words to loved ones such as our children, spouses or significant others. This is a time to mentally reflect on our role in what we have said, and as we are ready, to gently release. Let us mentally relax our cheek area, be aware of the smells through our nose. Move into our ear area, and take a look at what we may have heard. Some of us have experienced verbal abuse and as children we were powerless in terms of what we could select to hear. Go within and explore what we have heard. As you are ready, release and relax. Move into the eye area, and mentally be aware of anything we have seen as we were growing up. Some of us grew up in violent homes and saw people getting beaten up. This is a time for us to mentally take a look at what we experienced. And, as you are ready, to gently release and relax. Move into the top of our head, into our mind area. Let us be mentally aware of any thoughts we are holding, and as we are ready, to gently relax. Totally relax our bodies, our feelings, our spirits; to gently, gently be at peace with ourselves. Breathe in and gently breathe out.

As participants are ready, each is asked to pick up pencil and paper and to write a letter about what has come up for her or him during this relaxation.

Sufficient time is allowed for this process. Once this is completed, participants are placed in groups of three or four. Each member is asked to read his or her letter or writing to the others in the group. Aboriginal music is played during this time to allow a sense of familiarity.

There are often Aboriginal people who do not write. These folks will make up one group, where they will sit and talk about their experience.

After the group finishes this process, the ideal way to bring closure to this portion of the writing circle is to have the participants burn their letters. If that is not possible, then either collect the letters and burn them later, or ask the participants to burn their letters when they return home. Some participants may choose to take their letters to the grave of the loved one, or to send them to the person to whom they wrote.

Once this is finished, then participants are placed in groups of eight to ten for ice breakers, which helps bring positive closure. These ice breakers help Aboriginal people to heal in another way—which is through laughter.

Closure is brought through doing a version of a friendship circle using round-dance music. Two circles are formed. One dances clockwise, the other dances counter-clockwise. While dancing, participants are asked to offer a handshake or greeting. They are asked to dance for all of their spirit helpers who have seen them through their grieving.

CONCLUSION

Writing circles have been extremely successful with Aboriginal people. Using many affirmations, reinforcing that this is a safe place to be, giving permission to all present that they do not have to dot their *i*'s or cross their *t*'s—these approaches appear to work well in our communities.

In the process of reading their works, many Aboriginal people have become paralysed as they re-experience their pain of sexual abuse; some have vomited; some have curled up in a ball as a way of dealing with their pain. Others have built barricades of chairs to feel safe. Some have felt safe lying under a table. Whatever the process, it is their process. As each participant completes his or her journey, he or she comes back to the circle. Each person is not judged, but included.

It is most enlightening to see Aboriginal people telling their stories. It is through story that we let go of the pain. It is in letting go of the pain that we become free. It is in becoming free that we have choices. It is in having choices that we are able to guide our own destiny.

REFERENCES

Bass, Ellen and Laura Davis. (1988). *The Courage to Heal: A Guide for Women Survivors of Child Sexual Abuse.* New York: Perennial Library, Harper & Row.

Cajete, Gregory. (1994). *Look to the Mountain: An Ecology of Indigenous Education.* Durango, Colorado: Kivaki Press.

Cordova, Viola F. (1996). "Doing Native Philosophy." In Sylvia O'Meara and Douglas A. West, eds., *From Our Eyes: Learning from Indigenous Peoples*, pp. 13–18. Toronto:

As We See . . . Aboriginal Pedagogy 7

Garamond Press.

Grant, Agnes. (1990). *Our Bit of Truth: An Anthology of Canadian Native Literature.* Winnipeg, Manitoba: Pemmican Publications, Inc.

Hampton, Mary, Eber Hampton, Germaine Kinunwa and Lionel Kinunwa. (1995). "Alaska Recovery and Spirit Camps: First Nations Community Development." *Community Development Journal* 30: 257–264.

Hart, Michael Anthony. (1996). "Sharing Circles: Utilizing Traditional Practice Methods for Teaching, Helping, and Supporting." In Sylvia O'Meara and Douglas A. West, eds., *From Our Eyes: Learning from Indigenous Peoples*, pp. 59–72. Toronto: Garamond Press.

Walker, Alice. (1996). *The Same River Twice: Honoring the Difficult.* New York: Scribner.

White, Linda Odjig. (1996). "Medicine Wheel Teachings in Native Language Education." In Sylvia O'Meara and Douglas A. West, eds., *From Our Eyes: Learning from Indigenous Peoples*, pp. 107–122. Toronto: Garamond Press.

Wilson-Schaef, Anne. (1989) *Escape from Intimacy: The Pseudo-Relationship Addictions.* San Francisco: Harper & Row, Publishers.

Pedagogy from the Ethos: An Interview with Elder Ermine on Language

Willie Ermine

Introduction

During the fall of 1995, an 85-year-old Cree lady from the Sturgeon Lake Cree Nation passed into the spirit world. The significance of the old lady was, first of all, that she was a mother, a grandmother, a great-grandmother and a great-great-grandmother to many people. Secondly, her significance to me was that she was one of my mentors and also my "mother" as we understand our relationship in Cree kinship. In non-Native terms, she was my aunt. Finally, she held great significance because she had been one of the few remaining elders at Sturgeon Lake who had retained a traditional Cree world-view with rich perspectives of humanity passed on to her by the ancient people of our community.

The passing of Elder Ermine into the spirit world was a great loss to younger generations of knowledge seekers. Hers was the life of a traditional Cree woman living, growing and experiencing the ethos of a community modelled and developed by more ancient people in tune with timeless knowledge. Elder Ermine was guided on her own pathways of life and towards her own understanding and wisdom through perspectives untainted by Western thought. It is through this cultural mirror that Elder Ermine noticed the many changes affecting her own people during her lifetime; but, more importantly, she had seen the consistencies that held the community and its people together. The truth, as spelled out by Elder Ermine, arises from the consistencies of nature that she held so dearly and experienced so passionately during her lifetime. Her experience and insight into the community ethos guided her perceptions in old age and gave her the authority and responsibility to carry the truth and the teachings onward.

There are three purposes that drive this study. First, the major focus and intent of this exercise is driven by the search for ways to rejuvenate the Cree language. In this process, this paper examines the words arising from a thinker who has had life experiences and knowledge from the perspective of a traditional Cree world-view. The expectation is that those thoughts give insight to what informs the ethos of a community and what has driven the persistence of identity in the people. Transcribing Elder Ermine's words from Cree to English is a major part of the task of relaying the information to the wider public. The transcription is followed by the interpretation of the responses to the questions posed as part of the process of recording her wisdom.

Secondly, examining the words and wisdom of Elder Ermine also serves to illustrate the value of dialogue as an instrument in Aboriginal pedagogy. Dialogue will be defined, its value in the process of establishing and protracting relationships in pursuit of cultural knowledge will be discussed, and it will be used as an instrument in following traditional protocol for matters of cultural knowledge acquisition. Not only is dialogue an integral tenet in the oral tradition of the Cree culture, but its practice is also a commitment to follow the dictates of the ethos. Protocol continues to occupy prominence in Cree culture not only with respect to the aged ones of the community but also in matters pertaining to the community ethos. Therefore, part of the intent of this study is to make explicit the importance of protocol in the acquisition of information and knowledge in Cree culture.

The third objective of this study is to reflect on Aboriginal pedagogy and how Elder Ermine's insights and reflections from the ethos contribute to the development of pedagogy that empowers first language proponents. The scope of discussion in this paper will encompass the formation of an Aboriginal pedagogy in broader areas of language and culture.

THE RELATIONSHIP

Elder Ermine was a mother to me. In the Cree kinship, my father's brothers are my "fathers" in kinship and their wives are my "mothers" in kinship. Therefore, the association I have with Elder Mary is more profoundly that of a mother-child relationship with the same respectfulness and understandings as my own blood mother. The same relationship is also afforded to my "second fathers" as to my genetic father.

I had developed a very close relationship with my second father and second mother over the course of many years. Visits to their home were common during the course of the developing relationship. I came to see that the rapport I had developed with my second parents was respectfully grounded in the age-old tradition of a mentor-student dialogue and, more especially, as a parent-child relationship. My own yearning to know many of the ways of the Cree people and about the ethos of my own community had brought me to their home many an evening to listen to their words of reflection and guidance. Hughes has described the interview process as the "observation of people in situ; finding them where they are, staying with them in some role" (1960, p. 39) in order to allow for intimate observation and reporting that is not harmful. However, the purpose of the evening discussions was not to observe and report, but simply to hear fascinating narratives about the ethos of the community. What I continue to feel and believe is that very rich knowledge is contained in these relationships that many of my community and my generation continue to develop with the Old People in many communities. For me, the process of observing my mentors "in situ" was in itself a process of "coming to knowing" about myself and my people with many of the pieces of the knowledge puzzle being inserted one by one over many nights.

DIALOGUE

The manner by which I found myself "coming to knowing" as we sat and talked at the Old People's home was through the process of dialogue. Paulo Freire defined dialogue in his book *Pedagogy of the Oppressed* as the "encounter between men, mediated by the world, in order to name the world" (1970, p. 76). The tenets of dialogue, according to Freire, are the reflection for understanding and the commitment to act on the understanding. In hindsight, the evenings with the Old People were actually a continuing process of naming the world, and naming the community ethos in particular, for understanding and commitment to act. Freire goes on to state that dialogue cannot exist in the absence of profound love for the world and for humans. He states that dialogue has to have love, humility, hope, and intense faith in humans, along with the necessary engagement and critical thinking. These attributes encompassed the dialogue I had with the Old People.

THE COMMUNITY ETHOS

Elder Ermine had experienced the teachings and had experienced the truths as spelled out by the Old People in her community during the course of her 85 years. In her waning years of life, Elder Ermine talked with a passion about the ancient people and how they developed the ethos of our community. The ethos is the characteristic habits and attitudes of the totality that contributes to and creates the spirit of the home community. For Elder Ermine, the ethos was not only the inviolable spirit and community norms as built up by the ancient people before her time but also the essence and timeless knowledge that informs that construction of spirit. For Elder Ermine, the ethos became sacred because it contained the covenant that the people had with eternity and echoed the teachings of the ancient people before her time.

The ethos became the standard by which Elder Ermine constructed morality and how she shaped her truths as she reflected upon the mistakes she made in her own lifetime. She talked about those mistakes and how her years of acquired knowledge and wisdom had changed her perspectives. In an interview, she disclosed her perspectives and beliefs and stated that the responsibility of maintaining the ethos must be transmitted to the younger generations of the community. The consistencies or the truths that had taken her years to understand are the perimeters and the frameworks by which continuity of culture is to be maintained.

Cajete described the Indigenous community in the following terms:

In Indigenous communities the elders, the grandmothers and grandfathers, hold the stories of their families and their people. It is they who give the stories, the words of good thought and action to the children. They tell the children how the world and their people came to be. They tell the children of their experiences, their life. They tell them what it means to be one of the people. They tell them about their relationships to each other and to all things that are part of the world. They tell them about respect—just as their grandparents told them when they were children. So it goes, giving and receiving, giving and receiving stories—helping children remember to remember that the story of their community is really the story of themselves! [Cajete, 1994, p. 69]

Elder Ermine's words reflected this perspective well as she continually constructed the story that she lived and how the young must now try to construct their own life story.

Elder Ermine's experiences and insights, and her elderly status, allowed her to hold authority for Cree teachings and to be able to comment on what the truth is for our community. Elder Ermine's statement during the course of the interview that she did "not know anything" is not a disclaimer of authority. Walter Lightning has indicated that "this is a claim for the authority of the teaching, not for the authority of the Elder. . . . It is an implicit claim that the ethos is the origin of these teachings" (1992, p. 239). In what seems the most important context for the purpose of this study, it is these consistencies of ethos, elders, protocol and truths that informs the basis of an Aboriginal pedagogy in this paper.

THE INTERVIEW

The interview with Elder Mary Ermine took place on November 17, 1993, at her home. She lay on her bed because she had become sickly and was immobilized at the time of the interview. All of the dialogue was conducted in the Cree language, the only language that she knew. A tape recorder was used to record the interview. Only the relevant information was transcribed from Cree to English from that interview. The interview itself had an atmosphere of a discussion, an exchange, in the time-honoured tradition of reflective dialogue.

The questions posed to Elder Ermine were as follows:
1. How can a child learn to speak the language?
2. What can be done now that the children are losing their Cree language?
3. How about the school? Is that the proper place for children to learn the Cree language, or does it have to be the home?
4. Why are children losing their Cree language?

THE PROTOCOL

According to Walter Lightning in *Compassionate Mind*, protocol "refers to any one of a number of culturally ordained actions and statements, established by ancient tradition, that an individual completes to establish a relationship with another person from whom the individual makes a request." (1992, p. 216) The interview with Elder Mary Ermine involved a process of protocol. The process of requesting certain information or knowledge from elders involves a process of protocol in traditional Cree ways. In Cree tradition and in respect of that tradition, protocol maintains the ethos of the community in the transaction of information and knowledge. The ethos of the community is respected and is guided on the course of truth as it has been shown to the people. Lightning has said, "if one follows the protocols, in all of their explicitness, those truths remain forever" (1992, p. 241) and that teachings such as Elder Ermine's that have been obtained through protocol would not "power out, or lose energy" (1992, p. 242).

The request for the interview and the questions to be posed with Elder Ermine took place long before the interview itself. The primary purpose of the lead time to the interview was to allow for Elder Ermine to incubate her thoughts on the subject. At the time of the interview, I brought food for the Old People to eat prior to the actual questioning and dialogue. Tobacco and a prayer cloth were also given to Elder Ermine in respect for the request to "take" her traditional Cree knowledge.

ETHICAL SPACE

Poole has remarked in his book *Towards Deep Subjectivity* that there exists an "ethical space" when two sorts of space interact. Ethical space is created when the intentions of two entities structure the space between them in two different ways and when the two sets of intentions confront each other—"then ethical space is set up instantaneously" (Poole, 1972, p. 5). The interview with Elder Ermine was in the context of a philosophical understanding to try to maintain the Cree language, and both of our intentions were congruent in this regard. Clearly, Elder Ermine's wish was to keep the Cree language alive, and my primary purpose for the interview was to seek insights and information on how that could be accomplished. Where the creation of "ethical space" seemed to enter into the context of the interview was in the appropriateness of using traditional protocol for the purposes of creating text. The oral tradition of the Cree people maintains that the knowledge and teachings should be passed on by word of mouth and action-oriented transmission.

THE TEXT OF ELDER ERMINE'S WORDS

Q. How can a child learn to speak the Cree language?

[The child] has to be shown how. [The child] has to be shown how. But the child too, does not want to listen. Instead I am the one expected to speak English.

This is what the boys used to tell me.

My son used to contradict me. "We have to know English," he used to tell me. "Yes," I used to say to him, "you will know. There are two ways of speaking that you will try to learn. You should not lose your own way of speaking. Also, do not forget the English language that you are taught too. Do not lose your own way of talking," I used to say to him.

I have nothing in the way of schooling, just a little while. I do not know anything. I just use one language.

You are still getting an education. Take it, take it, in addition, take the Cree language.

Do not discard your own way of talking.

Oh, I used to talk profusely. In fact, the Old Man used to tell me, "Your words are annoying because of your constant talk to the boys." There were only boys, you know. "No, no," I told him. "I do not talk to annoy, I am doing the right thing, I am trying to raise my children. The children are trying to grow up," I told him. "They are men, they must try to grow up, to support themselves," I told him.

I was not supposed to do that, to annoy them. That is right anyway; there was never a time he strapped the boys, not once. There was one time he just about whipped one of the boys. Oh, my mother was really angry that he just about whipped him. But he had gone to swim at the little lake. That was him. But he didn't whip him, but he was close. Oh, my late mother was angry. She didn't like her grandchildren to be punished. That is all. That is about it. If there was ever a time that he whipped his children, never, nothing. Four girls, four girls, his children are lying here [in the grave], two boys, the one we lost most recently and one of our babies. In total we lost seven children. It is hard.

Q. What can be done now that the children are losing their Cree language?

They have to be told. There has to be continued effort to tell them, to show them how to speak Cree when you talk to them. To tell them to repeat your words. To continue your efforts to show them how. Not to discard the language that is your own way of talking. Do not throw it away, that is what you say to them. To tell the older people to tell their children, to tell their children, to keep up the effort. If they are not going to tell them anything, then I don't know about that. If the parents are not going to tell them anything.

Even that Old Lady, that Old Lady down by the clearing. I used to hear her. She used to think highly of children, my children, just as if they were her own grandchildren. She used to tell them things. She used to say to them, "Don't do that, don't do that, don't go and do improper things at other households." She used to say different things to them. She told them gently. I used to listen to her.

It is so, that you are told many things. You have taken those words and you have grown up gently, there is nothing disrespectful in the things done. Nothing much. Your mother has probably told you things while she was still alive. For me, however, I tended to speak angrily when I told the boys something. I was not supposed to do that. I am supposed to tell my children something in the gentle, quiet manner. That is the way. I tended to talk to them angrily, almost to the point of hitting them. That is not the way. Slowly, slowly. To take my words. Ah, it is hard.

My understanding is like this now. For example in how I notice my granddaughter. Although she mistreated her children. She talks gently to her boy. She talks slowly to him. She never hits him. I tell her once in a while here, for example right now, I am awaiting her arrival. "Don't ever talk angrily to the boy. Talk to him gently, don't hit him." I am going to tell her. All those things I am going to tell her, not to mistreat her children. If you talk angrily to a child, the child will not listen. The child will do worse. But, slowly, slowly telling the child, maybe they will listen to that.

It is mysterious, that our son, our baby, he was wise. He used to tell us things, but I guess that was because we were going to lose him, that he told us things. He used to pray, he used to pray for us. He really thought much of going to prayer. He could recite the readings, he knew the songs . . . mysterious. I found it amazing how he fully knew things. One time I was washing and we had set up a tent for him to stay in. For him to see if anybody was coming. I was alone. [My husband] was working. Then I secretly peeked in and there he was praying. That was our boy. He was seven when he left us. It is hard. He was quite big. He was seven years old. It is hard.

Q. How about the school? Is that the proper place for children to learn the Cree language, or does it have to be the home?

It would be good for them to be taught the Cree language there. Even to have one or two women to teach them. To teach the students in a separate place. Not to be taught constantly but to be occasionally separated to address the Cree language.

It is not good . . . I don't like to hear a child speaking English. Even older persons do that. [That person] does not look like a white person.

The one thing that I like. That is my land you know. That whole field, the size of it, that is my former husband's land. That and the pow-wow grounds, all that land, I would like for children to try to learn something there. The child should be taught everything on that land. That is the purpose of that land.

Q. Why are children losing their Cree language?

It is the fault of the older people. I would think. It is the same way I used to think in former times. I didn't like what I was thinking. I used to tell my son to teach his children to speak English, to tell them to speak English. When they came in, to teach them. But I was not doing the right thing. Not good. I was supposed to encourage that to my daughter-in-law. She was supposed to teach them the Cree language. To try to teach them the Cree language. There is a place to teach them how to speak English. When they got home, I told her, "Speak Cree to them. Speak Cree to them. There is a place for them to speak English."

But no, instead, she spoke English to them.

It is so, I used to speak angrily to these boys. "Don't speak like that; I don't understand you," I told them. "And when I speak Cree, you don't understand me. You should listen to me instead, anyway, there is a place where they can teach you, and it is for to talk to you in the Cree language. Listen to me," I used to tell them.

This Old Man, I never heard him talk to the children on these matters. That is what I used to tell him: "I never hear you speak to your children."

"It doesn't serve any purpose that you talk to them and they don't listen to you," he used to say to me. But no. Even if my children don't listen to me, I will still teach them something. If they don't take my spoken word, then it is up to them, I used to tell them. I have to tell my children something, I cannot just look at them when they act improperly, no, no. This is what I told him.

THE INTERPRETATION

[The child] has to be shown how. [The child] has to be shown how. But the child too, does not want to listen. Instead I am the one expected to speak English.

Elder Ermine is saying that, in order for a child to learn, role modelling has to take place for the benefit of the child. The child literally has to be shown how to do what is required of him or her. The value of role modelling as a popular tenet in Aboriginal education has been discussed by many people. Elder Ermine continues to say that learning has to be done mutually by the learner and the teacher. If one party does not have the motivation to learn, then learning cannot take place. Nor can learning take place out of context, that is, by talking English when Cree is the language to be learned. These statements reveal the distortion of ethos by the young people who require the older people to speak a language that does not properly belong to the ethos of the community.

My son used to contradict me. "We have to know English," he used to tell me. "Yes," I used to say to him, "you will know. There are two ways of speaking that you will try to learn. You should not lose your own way of speaking. Also, do not forget the English language that you are taught too. Do not lose your own way of talking," I used to say to him.

Elder Ermine realizes the value of learning two languages, as she indicates in this sequence of statements. There is clearly an emphasis on retaining the Aboriginal language and not sacrificing the first language while learning English. Elder Ermine clearly indicates that learning the two languages simultaneously ought to occur.

> I have nothing in the way of schooling, just a little while. I do not know anything. I just use one language.

The humility of elder teachers is present in these words of Elder Ermine. She uses the phrase "I do not know anything" in the age-old tradition of wise seers who understand the value and the dimensions of knowledge. Elder Ermine clearly illustrates the value of the Cree language in terms of attaining knowledge and the superficiality of using the English language for the sake of survival in our "modern world." Elder Ermine continued to survive quite well, even though she did not speak English. Lightning has said that such words indicate "a claim for the authority of the teaching, not for the authority of the Elder. . . . It is an implicit claim that the ethos is the origin of these teachings" (1992, p. 239).

> You are still getting an education. Take it, take it, in addition, take the Cree language.

She re-emphasizes that learning the English language does not mean that the original Cree language should be sacrificed. She stresses the importance of retaining the original language as part of the education process. Elder Ermine clearly states that the primal language identifies the person and is, in essence, the person.

> Oh, I used to talk profusely. In fact, the Old Man used to tell me, "Your words are annoying because of your constant talk to the boys." There were only boys, you know. "No, no," I told him. "I do not talk to annoy, I am doing the right thing, I am trying to raise my children. The children are trying to grow up," I told him. "They are men, they must try to grow up, to support themselves," I told him.

There are two ideas contained in this sequence of statements by Elder
Ermine. The first is that, in Elder Ermine's insistence that her boys will
listen to her, she crosses the fine line of being annoying rather than
processing actual teaching. These actions were detected by the "Old Man,"
who tells her of this fundamental flaw in her teaching method. The second
idea in these statements is that Elder Ermine, as the mother of the boys, is
trying to teach the boys values of life as part of the process of raising them.
The premise that the mother is the teacher of values in the household, even
when the father is present, is evident in these statements.

> I was not supposed to do that, to annoy them. That is right
> anyway; there was never a time he strapped the boys, not once.
> There was one time he just about whipped one of the boys. Oh, my
> mother was really angry that he just about whipped him. But he
> had gone to swim at the little lake. That was him. But he didn't
> whip him, but he was close. Oh, my late mother was angry. She
> didn't like her grandchildren to be punished. That is all. That is
> about it. If there was ever a time that he whipped his children,
> never, nothing. Four girls, four girls, his children are lying here [in
> the grave], two boys, the one we lost most recently and one of our
> babies. In total we lost seven children. It is hard.

Elder Ermine is using her past experience and the construction of her
story as examples that show right from wrong deeds. The process of
teaching children involves a delicate task of making holistic connections to
the child. Elder Ermine states from experience and hindsight that her
diatribes to the boys were a mistake and that that is not the way to teach
children. Further, she cites the example of the "Old Man" just about
whipping the boy: it takes the advice of an older woman, an older teacher
from the ethos, to tell them that such things are wrong to do in the process
of teaching children. This is an example of the learning that Elder Ermine
went through herself to arrive at her knowledge about teaching children.
Another thought in the whole process of teaching children is the value put
on children in the ethos of the community. Elder Ermine mentions that they
have seven children who passed away and it seems that scolding children
causes remorse when one realizes the value of their presence.

They have to be told. There has to be continued effort to tell them, to show them how to speak Cree when you talk to them. To tell them to repeat your words. To continue your efforts to show them how. Not to discard the language that is your own way of talking. Do not throw it away, that is what you say to them. To tell the older people to tell their children, to tell their children, to keep up the effort. If they are not going to tell them anything, then I don't know about that. If the parents are not going to tell them anything.

Elder Ermine is talking about the ethos and how the language of the community needs to be transferred to the younger people as part of ethos continuity. Loss of language creates the danger of loss of identity. Elder Ermine is not aware of what happens to the ethos in the event that the community chooses not to follow the language traditions.

Even that Old Lady, that Old Lady down by the clearing. I used to hear her. She used to think highly of children, my children, just as if they were her own grandchildren. She used to tell them things. She used to say to them, "Don't do that, don't do that, don't go and do improper things at other households." She used to say different things to them. She told them gently. I used to listen to her.

Elder Ermine's learning was from observing and listening to the older people in her community and her time. The ethos of the community is talking in these statements. The "Old People" from whom Elder Ermine received her teachings are still present to give the instructions. She clearly indicates in these statements that the proper behaviours and values were consistently taught to the children by other members of the community, and often through matriarchal lines. These statements suggest that the process of teaching children requires a gentle and amiable approach, like the approach of the "Old People."

It is so, that you are told many things. You have taken those words and you have grown up gently, there is nothing disrespectful in the things done. Nothing much. Your mother has probably told you things while she was still alive. For me, however, I tended to speak angrily when I told the boys something. I was not supposed

to do that. I am supposed to tell my children something in the
gentle, quiet manner. That is the way. I tended to talk to them
angrily, almost to the point of hitting them. That is not the way.
Slowly, slowly. To take my words. Ah, it is hard.

These statements again arise from the ethos of the community. Elder
Ermine makes the connection between myself and my mother as the line of
transfer from the ethos to the present. Any learning that arises from the
ethos requires a gentle transfer, a reflective pace so that the knowledge and
learning can be accomplished. Elder Ermine uses her own experience of
what is not done to violate the proper transfer of knowledge from the ethos
to the individual.

My understanding is like this now. For example in how I notice
my granddaughter. Although she mistreated her children. She talks
gently to her boy. She talks slowly to him. She never hits him. I tell
her once in a while here, for example right now, I am awaiting her
arrival. "Don't ever talk angrily to the boy. Talk to him gently,
don't hit him." I am going to tell her. All those things I am going to
tell her, not to mistreat her children. If you talk angrily to a child,
the child will not listen. The child will do worse. But, slowly,
slowly telling the child, maybe they will listen to that.

The responsibility to maintain the ethos of the community and to
transfer that knowledge rests with the older people. Elder Ermine has had
experiences and insights regarding how that could be done. As a
grandmother, she is now in the process of teaching her granddaughter about
the ways of raising and teaching children as it was always done.

It is mysterious, that our son, our baby, he was wise. He used to
tell us things, but I guess that was because we were going to lose
him, that he told us things. He used to pray, he used to pray for us.
He really thought much of going to prayer. He could recite the
readings, he knew the songs . . . mysterious. I found it amazing
how he fully knew things. One time I was washing and we had set
up a tent for him to stay in. For him to see if anybody was coming.
I was alone. [My husband] was working. Then I secretly peeked in
and there he was praying. That was our boy. He was seven when he

left us. It is hard. He was quite big. He was seven years old. It is
hard.

Elder Ermine is stressing the value of children to the parents and the
community. She mentions the giftedness of children, and their capacity and
potential to make contributions to humanity. This passage reveals how
Elder Ermine views spirituality as important to the community ethos, and
how the loss of one child is a loss to the whole of the community within
that context.

> It would be good for them to be taught the Cree language there.
> Even to have one or two women to teach them. To teach the
> students in a separate place. Not to be taught constantly but to be
> occasionally separated to address the Cree language.

The responsibility of the mother to teach the Cree language is evident in
these statements. There is the idea that the critical formula of the mother-
child relationship required in teaching the Cree language can be transferred
into the classroom to supplement the teaching at home. It suggests a vital
connection in the form of validation should be made between the home and
the school.

> It is not good . . . I don't like to hear a child speaking English.
> Even older persons do that. [That person] does not look like a
> white person.

This is statement a coming from the ethos. It suggests a critical loss of
identity for those persons from the community who prefer to speak English
within that environment. It suggests also a distortion of the ethos and the
insurmountable odds of failure in trying to be what one is not.

> The one thing that I like. That is my land you know. That whole
> field, the size of it, that is my former husband's land. That and the
> pow-wow grounds, all that land, I would like for children to try to
> learn something there. The child should be taught everything on
> that land. That is the purpose of that land.

These statements indicate the value of the land and the environment in the
education of children. She supposes that a living energy exists between the

land and the continuity of culture and learning.

> It is the fault of the older people. I would think. It is the same
> way I used to think in former times. I didn't like what I was
> thinking. I used to tell my son to teach his children to speak
> English, to tell them to speak English. When they came in, to teach
> them. But I was not doing the right thing. Not good. I was
> supposed to encourage that to my daughter-in-law. She was
> supposed to teach them the Cree language. To try to teach them the
> Cree language. There is a place to teach them how to speak
> English. When they got home, I told her, "speak Cree to them.
> Speak Cree to them. There is a place for them to speak English."
> But no, instead, she spoke English to them.

There is an explicit claim in these statements by Elder Ermine that the
teaching of the Cree language properly rests with the home environment. It
is the parents who have to teach their children how to use the language, and
if that does not happen then the parents and the older people are
responsible for the loss of the language. These statements explicitly say
that the mother has to teach the language. The ethos of the community
maintains that there needs to be continual impressions from the other
members of the community towards the use of the language.

> It is so, I used to speak angrily to these boys. "Don't speak like
> that; I don't understand you," I told them. "And when I speak Cree,
> you don't understand me. You should listen to me instead, anyway,
> there is a place where they can teach you, and it is for to talk to you
> in the Cree language. Listen to me," I used to tell them.

Elder Ermine is stressing that the home environment is the medium for
transferring the ethos and the language. She establishes that the mother is
the transmitter of the language and that the authority for that transmission
rests with the mother.

> This Old Man, I never heard him talk to the children on these
> matters. That is what I used to tell him: "I never hear you speak to
> your children."
> "It doesn't serve any purpose that you talk to them and they

don't listen to you," he used to say to me. But no. Even if my children don't listen to me, I will still teach them something. If they don't take my spoken word, then it is up to them, I used to tell them. I have to tell my children something, I cannot just look at them when they act improperly, no, no. This is what I told him.

Elder Ermine insists that children need guidance, and that perseverance should prevail to teach the ethos in the face of resistance and actions that work against the continuity of tradition.

The Pedagogy

The late Elder Ermine's words of wisdom are the source for the following pedagogy to rejuvenate the Cree language. Additionally, the process followed to obtain the information is juxtaposed with Elder Ermine's insights to create an overall pedagogy for cultural purposes. The following pedagogy, therefore, needs to be considered in the continuing development of Aboriginal learning processes and for rejuvenating the Cree language in particular. The pedagogy developed from the interview with Elder Ermine is as follows:

- The young people have to start developing relationships with the Old People of the community, who are the vital connections to understanding the ethos of the community.
- Dialogue has to be established and protracted with members of the community who hold insights into the ethos. Very often, it is the Old People of the community who hold the insights.
- Aboriginal pedagogy must contain the tenets of dialogue that are the reflection for understanding and the commitment to act on the understanding.
- Protocol has to be followed to access cultural knowledge. That knowledge is described by the Cree language.
- For a child to learn, role modelling has to take place for the benefit of the child. The child literally has to be shown how to do what is required of her or him. Children learn by observation, and adults have to set the example by using the language at home and outside the home. The actions have to be congruent with the words.
- If one party does not have the motivation to learn, then learning cannot

take place. The Cree language has to be presented as a dynamic and important language that has great relevance for Cree identity and understanding of the world. The community has to reward and recognize children's efforts to learn the language.

- Learning the Cree language cannot take place out of context. Teaching the language has to be done in the context of community dynamics. This is to say that teaching of the language within the confines of the classroom may be out of context.
- Retaining the Aboriginal language while at the same time learning the English language is important in the process of identity-building. Children's learning will be enhanced by the retention of their first language and learning the English language as a skill.
- There is an implicit claim that the ethos is the origin of Cree teachings. The rejuvenation of the Cree language must be approached by the community as a sacred act and the attributing of the spiritual element to guide the learning process.
- Retaining the original language is an important part of the education process. The children have to know who they are first by way of the Cree language before a foreign language and skills are introduced.
- It is crucial to teach the values of life as part of the process of raising children. The early years when children are being brought up are the most critical period in which the children have to be taught values, morality and the importance of retaining the Cree language.
- The mother is the teacher of values in the household. It is important that the schooling process does not impinge on children's development of values.
- It is important in Aboriginal pedagogy to use personal experience in the construction of personal story as examples that show right from wrong deeds. The first language will enhance the children's construction of their own life stories and how to name the world.
- The process of teaching children involves a delicate task of making holistic connections to the child. Building trusting relationships and approaching the learning process from the heart, mind, emotion and intellect is important in Aboriginal pedagogy.
- Loss of identity occurs when language is lost. The language names the world for the child and creates the vital personal connection to the

world and the processes at play in that world.

- Proper behaviours and values were consistently taught to the children by other members of the community, and often through matriarchal lines. The community has to take responsibility for the education of all the children in subjects that are important to the community. The ancient pedagogy where the female lines of kinship were responsible for the teaching of values have to be considered in models of education.

- The process of teaching children requires a gentle and amiable approach, as was the approach of the "Old People." The act of whispering and making the teachings almost mystical is a pedagogy that needs further consideration.

- The responsibility to maintain the ethos of the community and to transfer that knowledge rests with the older people.

- A vital connection in the form of validation can be made between the home and the school. What is taught in the school should enhance what is taught in the home.

- The value of the land and the environment should be emphasized in the education of children.

- The responsibility for teaching the Cree language properly rests with the home environment. It is parents who have to teach their children how to use the language and if that does not happen then the parents and the older people are responsible for the loss of the language. The school should give back the responsibility for teaching the language to the parents. Elder Ermine explicitly states that it is the mother who has to teach the language.

- Perseverance is needed to teach the ethos in the face of resistance and actions that work against the continuity of tradition.

SUMMARY

In summary, three purposes motivated this study. First, this paper's major focus and intent was to search for ways to rejuvenate the Cree language. In this process, this paper examined the words arising from a thinker who has had life experiences and knowledge from the perspective of a traditional Cree world-view. The expectation is that those thoughts give insight to what informs the ethos of a community and what has driven the persistence of identity in the people. The translation of Elder Ermine's words from Cree into English was a major part of the task of relaying the information to the wider public. Translation was followed by the interpretation of the responses to the questions posed as part of the process of recording her wisdom.

The second major purpose of this paper was to examine the words and wisdom of Elder Ermine in order to illustrate the value of dialogue as an instrument in Aboriginal pedagogy. Dialogue was defined and its value in the process of establishing and protracting relationships in pursuit of cultural knowledge was discussed. Dialogue was presented as an instrument in following traditional protocol for matters of cultural knowledge acquisition. Not only is dialogue an integral tenet of the oral tradition of the Cree culture, its practice is also a commitment to follow the dictates of the ethos. Protocol continues to occupy prominence in Cree culture not only with respect to the aged ones of the community but also in matters pertaining to the community ethos. Therefore, part of the intent of this study is to make explicit the importance of protocol in the acquisition of information and knowledge in Cree culture

The third objective of this study was to reflect on Aboriginal pedagogy and how Elder Ermine's insights and reflections from the ethos contribute in the development of pedagogy that empowers first language proponents. The scope of discussion in this paper was the basis for formation of an Aboriginal pedagogy in broader areas of language and culture.

REFERENCES

Cajete, G. (1994). *Look to the Mountains*. Durango, Colorado: Kivaki Press.

Freire, Paulo. (1970). *Pedagogy of the Oppressed*. New York: The Seabury Press.

Hughes, E. (1960). "Introduction: The Place of Fieldwork in Social Sciences." In B. Junker, ed., *Fieldwork*, pp. 39. Chicago: University of Chicago Press.

Lightning, Walter. (1992). "Compassionate Mind: Implications of a Text Written by Elder Louis Sunchild." *Canadian Journal of Native Education* 19: 215–253.

Poole, R. (1972). *Towards Deep Subjectivity*. London: The Penguin Press.

PLANTS AND MEDICINES:
AN ABORIGINAL WAY OF TEACHING

BENTE HUNTLEY

In North America today people are realizing that we have not
listened well, that we have neglected our relations on this Earth and
that Native American stories hold power and wisdom for helping
us learn how to live in balance with other forms of life. Through
the lessons of ecology—the study of the relationships between
living things and their environments—we have reaffirmed the
ancient knowledge of the stories. Science and myth may offer
different ways of viewing the world, but they teach us the universal
truth that there is an empirically obvious relationship between
people and Earth: we should not pollute and destroy our Mother,
our Provider, rather we should nurture and protect her. The lessons
for survival today come from listening to the old stories and from
studying the laws of how natural systems sustain themselves.
[Caduto and Bruchac, 1991a, p. 4]

INTRODUCTION

Aboriginal pedagogy, our own world-view and teachings, served the
needs of Aboriginal peoples for thousands of years before the arrival of a
new and dominant pedagogy (Burger, 1990; Cajete, 1994; Deloria, 1991;
Ermine, 1995; Isbister, 1993; Suzuki and Knudston, 1992). For centuries,
Aboriginal peoples relied on the oral traditional knowledge of their
environment for survival. Through observation and experience, Aboriginal
peoples the world over developed highly organized systems and knowledge
about plants and medicines. There are many Aboriginal cultures, not only
around the world, but here in Canada as well. However, I know, from my
contacts with other Aboriginal people from Canada and across the world,
that there exist common threads that weave us together. Steve McFadden,
author of *The Little Book of Native American Wisdom*, says that "the native

people of America hold common traditions of democracy and spiritual development that reach back tens of thousands of years" (McFadden, 1994, p. 5). These common threads are at the core of Aboriginal pedagogy and must be reinforced in our children in order to heal our fragile planet.

For the past century or more, traditional knowledge was condemned as "heathen" or "folklore," but Aboriginal peoples' traditional teachings and knowledge are, at long last, being recognized as valid and valued. It is the resilience of Aboriginal peoples, the world over, that has kept alive their oral traditions and teachings. Traditions and knowledge have long been underground and dormant, but many people are now starting to remember the grandfathers' and grandmothers' stories.

This paper focuses on two issues: the importance of the history and oral stories of traditional environmental knowledge; and a rationale for an ethnobotanical module for the classrooms. Through literature reviews and interviews the importance of traditional environmental knowledge will be explored, as will the implications and implementation of an ethnobotanical module for the schools. Finally, a list of resources (books, articles, tapes, people) will be provided. It is hoped that the oral stories and knowledge of and about Aboriginal peoples will create more positive attitudes, both in classrooms and in communities, toward Aboriginal peoples and their contributions to society.

I know what I know! But how do I know what I know? When I started the research on traditional environmental knowledge and asked the questions "What is the nature of Aboriginal epistemology?" and "How did Aboriginal peoples attain their knowledge of plants?" and more importantly "What does it mean?" (Deloria, 1991, p. 30), my curiosity was aroused. I began to learn about the nature of Aboriginal knowledge, what Suzuki and Knudtson (1992) call "the native mind" and, more importantly, I remembered the stories and lessons I had picked up throughout my life journey. I continue that journey with the knowledge and histories of my Cree grandmother and great-grandfather who introduced me to the fascinating world of plants and stories. Because of them, I have developed an interest in the knowledge of the old ones.

After completing a course in Renewable Resources Technology at Kelsey Institute, Saskatoon, I worked for the Forestry Branch in Prince

Albert. This gave me the opportunity to travel extensively throughout northern Saskatchewan, and this experience, along with the challenge of raising children, led me to the field of education. With my combined background in education and resources, I graduated with a renewed interest in natural science education and an awareness of the "crisis" in education.

There is an educational and ecological crisis according to Gregory Cajete, who states in his book *Look to the Mountain: An Ecology of Indigenous Education*:

> While the legacy of American education is one of spectacular scientific and technological achievement resulting in abundant material prosperity, the cost has been inexorably high. American prosperity has come at the expense of the environment's degradation and has resulted in unprecedented exploitation of human and material resources worldwide. [Cajete, 1994, p. 25]

This "prosperity" has come not only at the expense of the environment, but Aboriginal peoples as well. Children of Aboriginal heritage need to reaffirm that their culture, their stories, their knowledge and their history have value. As Cuduto and Brochac state, "stories are the living legacy of a people by which the wisdom of the ages is passed to each new generation" (Caduto and Brochac, 1994, p. 4). Since Aboriginal peoples see themselves interconnected to nature, "their stories use natural images to teach about relationships among people, plants and the rest of Earth" (Caduto and Bruchac, 1994, p. xviii). Through the development of culturally based and culturally sensitive curriculum, perhaps this reaffirmation can be accomplished. Indeed, the world needs to strive for new ways to heal the earth and her people.

METHODOLOGY

To get a deeper understanding of another way of knowing and learning, I decided to go to the sources of knowledge: medicine people and elders. A number of elders and experts on traditional knowledge were interviewed. These participants were actively involved from beginning to end, and they gave final approval for the project. Interviews were held with Sally Milne, Cecily Brass, Elder Vicki Wilson and the Reverend James Isbister. In most cases, detailed field notes were taken; the exceptions are noted later. The interviews varied from two to four hours. Due to the nature of the topic, the main questions (see Appendix) varied from individual to individual. In addition, many questions arose during the interviews themselves. Participants will be revisited to obtain (with permission) oral stories for the module.

The teachings of Aboriginal peoples were passed down orally, particularly through stories. They were, and continue to be, an integral part of Aboriginal cultures. Cajete feels that

> the ability to use language through storytelling, oratory, and song was highly regarded by all tribes as a primary tool for teaching and learning. This was because the spoken or sung word expressed the spirit and breath of life of the speaker and thus was considered sacred. [Cajete, 1994, p. 33]

It is, indeed, an ancient pedagogy, even though the written word is relatively new to Aboriginal peoples, and still foreign to some. More people the world communicate via oral language than via print. As Alexander Wolfe, a Saulteux storyteller and author of *Earth Elder Stories*, informs us,

> information and instruction were transmitted to us orally, in story form, by our old people. . . . If we are to preserve the stories that contain our history we must restore the art, practice and principles of oral storytelling. [Wolfe, 1988, p. xv]

Oral recordings and stories about plants will provide an introduction to Aboriginal ways of knowing, and explain how Aboriginal people identified, used and valued plants from their surroundings. If schools are ever going to succeed in creating positive self-images in Aboriginal students, then "a 'renewed tradition' in the bringing of traditional principles to contemporary focus" (Katz and St. Denis, 1991, p. 33) is needed. The interviews were a first step in that direction.

THE INTERVIEWS

SALLY MILNE

The first interview was with Sally Milne. On Monday morning, August

22, 1994, I set out to interview Sally Milne, a Cree woman from La Ronge, Saskatchewan. I first met her in 1990, when she was working at the Curriculum Resource Unit, developing local traditional curriculum for the Lac La Ronge Indian Band. She was considered one of the local experts on the traditional knowledge of Aboriginal arts and crafts. At the time, I was teaching grades 6, 7 and 8 (multi-grade classroom) at Sally Ross School in Hall Lake, one of the Lac La Ronge Indian Band schools. I invited Sally to the school (situated at Kiolmetre 46 on the Besnard Lake Road) for two days to show the students some traditional arts and crafts. Sally taught the students fish scale art, birchbark biting and moose hair tufting.

She started with fish scale art. While the children worked on their art pieces, Sally discussed and explained the procedures. The most interesting part, for me, was learning that the colours used for dying the fish scales came from natural dyes—mostly from plants. For example, the reds were obtained from various berries such as raspberries or cranberries, the purples came from chokecherries and the blues from blueberries and saskatoons— all berries with which the children were familiar. As well, Sally informed me she starts workshops with fish scale art because it is easier for the students. She works her way up to moose hair tufting (using the dyes from the same plants). "This," Sally stated, "teaches children patience." Cajete refers to these types of teachings, where morals and values are taught by community members, as key elements of Indigenous education (1994, p. 172).

After fish scale art, Sally explained the art of birchbark biting. Long before the Europeans arrived on this continent, birchbark was used to create patterns for quill, leather and tufting because the people did not have pen and ink. The students found this intriguing. Sally insisted that the students know the importance of taking only the outer bark of the birch trees to prevent the cambium from being destroyed, which would kill the tree. Of course, this led to a discussion about respect for all living things and "how our ancestors relied heavily on birchbark" (Milne, 1990). Respect for the environment and "all our relations" is another key element of Indigenous education, as stated by Cajete (1994, p. 174). Further patience was needed for birchbark bitings, because the bark had to be peeled to one thin layer. Many students were quite frustrated with the process, but eventually everyone created some bitings. Some students were much better at peeling the birchbark and volunteered to do some for the others who were not as patient.

The third and final craft Sally taught the students was moose hair tufting, and this art took the most patience and skill. Not many students finished their small pieces. The same plants were used to dye the moose hair, and Sally used the opportunity to explain how the plants were collected and used for the dyes.

After this visit, I worked with Sally developing the new science curriculum for the Lac La Ronge Indian Band. She was involved in all subject areas, integrating Aboriginal knowledge across the curriculum. It was during the science curriculum meetings that I began to understand the depth of knowledge Sally possessed about local plants. Since I was also interested in plants, we had a common bond. Years later, when I wanted to contact people about traditional environmental knowledge, especially ethnobotanical knowledge, Sally Milne came immediately to mind.

It was with a sense of excitement and anticipation that I set out for La Ronge one Monday morning. When I informed Sally about my project, she was both enthusiastic and concerned—enthusiastic because she felt, as I do, that our children are losing any sense or knowledge about plants and their uses. Sally knew a module for use in the classroom would help. She was concerned because she felt that children cannot even recognize the trees around them: "If you asked most of them to bring you a spruce bough they'd bring you a poplar branch" (Milne, 1994). It is also a concern raised and shared by many other people who study Aboriginal knowledge (McIvor, 1995; McFadden, 1994; Cajete, 1994; Suzuki and Knudston, 1992; and Burger, 1994).

Sally was also concerned about writing down the knowledge that Aboriginal medicine women and men had and continue to have. She feels, as I do, that knowledge must be transmitted the way it always has been for generations. The oral tradition is an important part of traditional environmental knowledge and must not be lost. This is, as Suzuki and Knudtson (1992) maintain, a fundamental difference from Western science. Sally's views about the passing on of the knowledge to those who have been selected or chosen is reflected by many others. According to Charlotte Erichsen-Brown, ethnobotanist and author of *Medicinal and Other Uses of Northern American Plants*, medicine people spent years learning their skills (1979, p. xii). Kahlee Keanne, also known as Root Woman, claims that knowledge passed on began early for chosen candidates and that:

> selection was from the family or from signs of devotion, wisdom and honesty. It was more than a career, as in our time, he [she] was elected by ability. Trusted with all secrets, rituals, habits and legends of their people, while attending all ceremonial celebrations and critical meetings of the people he [she] was at the side of their leader. The trainee must know and remember the many herbal species, their properties and uses. They knew their limitations and that flowers of the garden are not an agent against the fate of death, but there are flowers for sickness and health and flowers to prolong life. All medicinal plants in the area were used. The flora and fauna differed in each locality, but each knew their immediate supply. [Brown-Erichsen, 1979, p. xxvii]

Sally also discussed what she calls "common knowledge," the knowledge that is common to both Aboriginal and non-Aboriginal people. This is the knowledge that I possess. For example, many people know that ratroot is used for sore throats. As a matter of fact, many people I know from the La Ronge area always carry a supply of ratroot with them wherever they go.

At a recent conference I attended in Saskatoon, I ran into a wonderful woman I had met while working for the La Ronge Band. I happen to be allergic to cigarette smoke and, although the conference rooms were smoke-free, the lobby was not. I therefore developed a severely sore throat and kept clearing my throat as I talked. My friend, Kate Hamilton (who is also a wonderful storyteller and has tremendous knowledge of plants and their uses), pulled out a long piece of ratroot, broke off a chunk and told me to chew and suck on it. I did. After a few minutes, my throat felt much better. At least I could swallow.

As well as ratroot, Sally showed me another plant well known to most people for its medicinal value: the bark of willow, which is good for fevers. Sally mentioned a few more plants already familiar to me as valuable medicinal plants. But where did this knowledge come from? As Sally claims, it is common knowledge and is passed down orally, from generation to generation.

As we talked, I asked her why she was no longer working for the La Ronge Band. She informed me that she was caring for her ailing mother, but that she was also a student. I had not realized it when I set out to interview Sally: she was on the path to becoming a traditional healer. I was surprised and amazed. My question about whether or not there were many traditional shamans or medicine men or women left was answered without my asking, and I was relieved to know the tradition was still being carried on. Sally informed me that there is not only a renewed interest by our people, but many, many candidates as well.

I felt, as Sally felt, that any knowledge must be passed on in the traditional manner. Even though it is extremely important for everyone to understand and accept the value of traditional environmental knowledge, the specific knowledge of the medicine lodge must be kept sacred, as it always has been in the past. Sally felt very uncomfortable if I took notes, so I did not, and much of what I learned from her will not be transmitted here. There is a time and place for such knowledge, and here and now is not the place. It was reassuring to know that Sally felt, as I do, that the oral traditions must be kept alive and the sacred traditions kept sacred. I thank Sally Milne for her candid insight and her wise advice, so that my journey, which began so many years ago, can and will continue far into the future.

CICELY BRASS

Another interview, with Cicely Brass, was held on September 16, 1994. Cicely is my aunt and lives in Davis, Saskatchewan. She was 65 years old. Aunt Cicely grew up on Muskoday Reserve, about 15 miles southeast of Prince Albert. She is married, with nine children. Cicely remembered some of the stories from her childhood and a couple of women who knew quite a bit about plants. Her aunt, Alice Crain, was one of those women, but, to my aunt's recollection, she never passed her knowledge on to anyone. I also discovered that Edward Dreaver's grandmother was a medicine woman. Apparently she knew and collected all sorts of medicines: Cicely recalled watching her going out into the bush and fields on a daily basis. I wondered if many people went to her for healing. Cicely remembers quite a few people visiting the medicine woman for a variety of health reasons. Because doctors were far away at that time, Aboriginal people still relied on the knowledge and wisdom of their medicine people.

I wondered how my aunt learned to recognize certain plants, and she informed me that her father (my great-grandfather) showed her. He knew just about everything about plants, how to recognize them and the uses they had. "We just got so we'd recognize the plants. We were quite young, I was about seven, everybody would go out and pick." My aunt learned by "keen personal observations and experiences" (Suzuki and Knudtson, 1992). I asked my aunt about some of the stories she remembered about plants and plant knowledge.

Dad used to start many fires with birchbark. He used to carry it in his pocket all the time, when he went out to the trapline. I don't remember dad using willow for anything, but I do know we used sinew from cows tendons to sew moccasins. Of course, my mother used to can saskatoons, high and low bush cranberries, strawberries and raspberries. We used to mush choke cherries between two rocks, add some sugar and eat them with cream. I know that my dad said that rosehips were good for cold prevention [very high in vitamin C]. Great grandpa Henry used to make pipes out of wood, from a tree—but I don't remember what kind of tree. But he used to smoke the inner bark of red willow. He used to pull out the inner bark and mix it with other tobacco, usually Club. He lived until he was 105 years old.

Oh, and I remember picking the sap off spruce trees and we would chew it like gum. [This reminds me of peeling the inner pith of a small plant and chewing it like gum.] Let's see. Barley grass was good for arthritis. Mom used to take a plant leaf, pull off the veins and put it on sores. It was a healing plant but I don't know the name of it. Cattails are good for healing. You take the spike, mix it with grease or lard to make a poultice, and put it on a burn or cut.

I remember once when I cut my leg real bad. That was when the doctors were too far away and all we had was horses to travel. My mother put a cattail poultice on my leg and it brought out the infection. Wish I knew more. It's amazing how we've lost our knowledge; there is so much we don't know about the plants anymore.

VICKI WILSON

The third interview was held October 25, 1994, with Elder Vicki Wilson. Vicki is an elder who works at the Wonska Cultural School in Prince Albert. She is a wise traditional woman. I informed her of my project and she was more than willing to talk to me. I asked her about the knowledge of the old ones and how they came to this knowledge. Vicki stated that it was through necessity: our ancestors had to survive on this continent through observation, trial and error. She knows of the strong connections Aboriginal people had (and still have) with the natural world and the importance of passing the knowledge gained down from generation to generation.

Vicki claimed that family traditions, dreams and visions also played a critical role in Aboriginal epistemology and pedagogy.

Birchbark was commonly used. [A story of Vicki's is included in the module.] Gramma used lots of herbs. She used to make small bundles of plants in medicine bags. She knew by the feel and smell just what it was for. Gramma instructed my mom. She couldn't remember though so she used to wrap and tag things. Someone stole it. The moral is that you weren't suppose to identify and tag the medicines because they were sacred gifts. The medicine bundles also had to be left outside for her own safety. The medicine had to be protected against women who came in their moontime, or a man who came with a bad heart and thoughts. These things affected the medicines. Because my mom forgot so much and was punished, I didn't get to learn about the herbs. Although I do have some of the common knowledge. I remember a purple prickly plant used for headaches. It could be made into a drink or mushed up and rubbed on the head. The inner bark of willow was also used for fevers and colds. There was a type of axle grease used on wagons, in tin containers, that was used to treat horses if they had a cut. I always wondered what was in the grease. I don't remember the adults ever getting sick but us kids often got colds. I wish I could remember more.

JAMES ISBISTER

The final interview was held in December, 1995, with the Reverend James Isbister. This interview was extremely interesting because Rev. Isbister is an Anglican minister who combines his "Christian" religion with his Aboriginal spirituality. The journey he undertook speaks about the resilience of Aboriginal peoples and their struggle to come to terms with the world in which we now live. I have known Rev. Isbister for many years because he was married to my half-sister for over 25 years. He became a minister about 21 years ago. He often wondered about mixing his cultures and told me that on his journey he learned how to handle the teachings of both and never rejected either. It has always been (and continues to be) tough. He feels Aboriginal priests like himself act as catalysts in many ways to build bridges between the two cultures. He had to walk in both worlds and has been stepped on and criticized, but he sees joy and enlightenment at the end of the tunnel. He now sees people coming out, mostly the middle-aged, practising the old ways. He feels (as so many others do) that the Elders and medicine people still hold many of the secrets of plants. The following are some of Rev. James Isbister's stories and insights into Aboriginal knowledge.

> I was very open when I was growing up. The Elders used to pick on me. They used to tell me things. I used to hear all the stories, the sacred stories about "magical places." You see the knowledge was passed down to those who were interested or gifted. And if an offering of tobacco is given to the Elders, then they are obligated to give you information. Tobacco is the entry into wisdom. It is profound because the smoke goes to God or the Creator. Elders never question, they understand and listen to you.
>
> The old ways are slowly coming back. They were never lost because of the rich way things were done, holistically. For instance, you must always ask permission from God or the Creator and the plants before you use it. Give a gift in return. Give a prayer to the plant thanking it for giving its life for you. This shows the interconnectedness and respect for all living things [Cajete's "all my relations"]. Never pick an over abundance of any plant, only

take what is needed. It is changing a little now because "Indian doctors" are picking more and storing them. Jacob Sanderson is a medicine man and he has a whole storehouse of herbs that he uses. But still he picks carefully and with respect. Because the plants sacrifice their lives, this relationship with all relatives is considered spiritual. They have given their spirit for you; it's hard to explain but it is something that is accepted and something that is lived. There is a cleansing and purification involved. And because I was so involved in "Native spirituality," it was easy to make the transition to Christian religion. The names don't matter. It is the same, the interconnectedness, the life giving, the passing of life. Perhaps that is why Christianity was so easy for our people to accept. It really was not that different. However, our oral traditions had gone underground for so long but now a lot of people are starting to remember what the Grandfathers knew. The spiritual part is starting to be realized; it was never lost, just sort of dormant. Because the fear has been taken away, now it's okay to come forward. Now it's okay to be what we have always strived to be. The Elders must lead the way but some might still be scared and protective about their medicines and knowledge. That's okay. It has been a challenge for me. I look forward to the future.

This ended my interviews to date. I intend to carry out many more. The interviews also provided me with many contacts for further research. The journey continues.

THE MODULE

CURRICULUM IMPLICATIONS

The literature in the field, the voices of the elders and the failure rate of Aboriginal students cry out for changes to the education system. A number of documents also support and acknowledge the need for culturally relevant materials in the education system (Northern Education Task Force Report, 1989; Indian and Metis Education Advisory Committee Report, 1992; Hart, 1987; Studies in Science Education, 1994; Science Curriculum Guide for the Elementary Level, 1990; Draft Declaration of Indigenous Rights, 1993). Indeed, the Indian and Metis Education Advisory Committee (1992) recommends that "curriculum material projects to support new curriculum initiatives be undertaken to provide materials not commercially available." A science module on plants must therefore be created to fulfil the above recommendations, to localize the "content of the science curriculum," and to make science "more relevant to the immediate experience and lives of students from generally under-represented groups" (Pomeroy, 1994, p. 7).

Units need to be developed that not only provide for the needs of Aboriginal students, but also focus on the contributions of Aboriginal people. What better way for Aboriginal people to gain self-respect, self-confidence and self-esteem? In this way, the curriculum will not only concentrate on the positive aspects of Aboriginal cultures, but will reinforce and validate the beliefs, values and traditions of Aboriginal cultures.

RATIONALE

The rationale behind a module on plants is twofold. First, plants are an integral part of the elementary science curriculum. Every grade focuses on some aspect of plants, whether it is plant structure and function (grade 5), plant growth (grade 2) or adaptations (grade 8). Second, plants were, and continue to be, a vital link to Aboriginal people's survival and culture. Therefore, Aboriginal content can easily be incorporated into the curriculum; that is, if the materials are available.

The module on plants, in keeping with the oral traditions and Aboriginal values, must be presented visually (slides) and orally (tapes). In addition, the tapes must include stories that link plants and people. Accompanying the slides and tapes will be ideas on how to incorporate the materials for each grade level. For example, the grade 1 unit on plants concentrates on how we use plants. The slides and corresponding tapes will discuss the value and uses of plants to Aboriginal people in general terms (i.e., berry or fruit plants, root plants, leaf plants); these plants can then be compared to the plants with which they are familiar. Along with the slides and tapes, a list of resources and a list of contact people will be provided so that teachers will adapt the module to their needs. An overall rationale and introduction will be presented both in written and oral format.

The value of traditional environmental knowledge and stories, especially the ethnobotanical knowledge, cannot be underestimated or undervalued. Traditional environmental knowledge contains the history, the ways of knowing, and the values and contributions of Aboriginal people worldwide. It is not a "new" way of thinking but is "and always will be, the precious life-sustaining property of First Peoples" (Suzuki and Knudston, 1992, p. 22). And "those who deny that living remnants of ancient aboriginal world view still persist, speak in ignorance" (Suzuki and Knudston, 1992, p. xxxiv). Therefore, the implications for the curriculum are astoundingly positive, even though the implementation will be a slow process.

IMPLEMENTATION

Curriculum materials need approval from Saskatchewan Education before they are put in the hands of the teacher. The module needs to be completed, field-tested, revised, retested and handed to a curriculum committee for approval. However, I know from my experiences working in the north for band schools that there is a constant demand for culturally relevant materials; so perhaps that is where one could start. Saskatchewan Education is always a few paces slower, and I know that the module could take months to create. Participatory research takes time and, when working with elders, the Western view of time has no meaning. I will learn what needs to be learned when the time is appropriate.

SAMPLE

The following is a sample of what might be recorded on the tapes.

Slides:

- white birch (*Betula papyrifera*; Cree name *waskway*)
- close-up of birchbark
- birchbark basket/birchbark bitings/birchbark canoe
- stripping a birch tree
- birch sapping
- smoking fish/meat with birch shavings

Tapes:

- history and value

Paper or white birch is one of the most versatile plants available to the Cree people (first slide). The bark was used in a variety of ways because it is lightweight, waterproof and abundant. The bark can be cut to any shape required, whether thin strips (next slide) are needed for bandages, fire starter or bitings, or whether larger sheets are needed for baskets, containers, canoes or tip coverings (next slide). Care must be always taken so the tree is not permanently damaged. If the whole tree is not used and just the bark taken, then the bark must not be peeled down to the cambium because it will kill the tree (next slide). In addition, an offering (tobacco is the most common) should be made whenever any plant or animal gives its life for our use.

The wood is used in a variety of ways. Because it is strong and tough, it is used to make paddles, snowshoes, toboggans, spoons, etc. The birch also has edible parts. The sap can be taken from the tree in the spring (in birchbark baskets) or the root can be boiled for a hot drink (next slide). In addition, the rotten or punky wood can be used to tan hides or powder baby bottoms. The wood-shavings also make great-tasting smoked fish and meat (next slide). Medicinally, birch tea made from the leaves is a diuretic, anti-inflammatory, antiseptic, tonic (Keanne, 1994; Leighton, 1986).

• identification

Waskway is easily recognized by its distinct whitish papery bark that peels off in layers. The bark is smooth and often has dark lines running horizontally across the trunk. *Waskwayak* are often arranged in clumps of three trees or more. From a distance, in the spring and summer, the crown appears reddish. *Waskway* is common throughout northern Saskatchewan.

• stories

> I was waiting to go to a dance, waiting for the horses to come. I made tea for my grandma; I dropped and fell sideways. The tea splashed and I burned my leg badly; but I went to the dance anyway. The next morning I was really sore. My grandma put thin layers of paper birchbark on my wound and left it overnight. It healed. If you put it on right away, it is not supposed to leave a scar. My scar is not too bad. [Elder Vicki Wilson, 1994]

CONCLUSION

A vital document that deals with Aboriginal rights with respect to epistemology and pedagogy is the Coolangatta Statement of 1993, drafted for the World's Indigenous Peoples Education Conference (cited as Draft Declaration of Indigenous Rights). The aim of the statement was to provide "a document that can be put to use by individuals, communities and nations throughout the world in their struggle to establish education systems which reflect and embrace the cultural values, philosophies and ideologies that have shaped and guided Indigenous peoples for thousands of years" (Draft Declaration of Indigenous Rights, 1993, p. 2). As a result of this conference, a final document on Indigenous rights to Indigenous education will be submitted to the United Nations before the year 2000.

Some main points of concern were voiced at the conference by all of the working groups involved (elders, educators, community and youth). One was that the language of the document must come from "the grassroots." It was also felt that we, as Indigenous peoples, possess all of the knowledge and expertise to develop such a document. In addition, the common consensus was that the most important aspects of Indigenous learning are our oral traditions; all Indigenous people use song, art, music, dance or stories in their learning, and it is essential that these be carried on for future generations. It was felt that Indigenous people have the inherent right to be educated in their own languages; the *true* histories and use of Indigenous perspectives must be recognized as valid. It is time to get rid of the "cultural bomb" (wa'Thiongo, 1986) that imperialism and colonialism has wielded against Aboriginal peoples the world over. The effect, indeed, has been to "annihilate a people's belief in their names, in their languages, in their environment, in their heritage of struggle, in their unity, in their capabilities and ultimately in themselves" (wa'Thiongo, 1986, p. 3). The cultural genocide must cease.

Cajete states that "education for Indian people has been, and continues to be, a grand story, a search for meaning, an essential food for the soul" (1994, p. 28). The schooling of our children has not worked well from a Western pedagogical viewpoint. And, as McIvor emphasizes, "our peoples have not vanished, nor has our traditional knowledge" (1995, p. 86). Saskatchewan's new core curriculum focuses on a more holistic approach to teaching, for the benefit of all children, so there is a place for both epistemologies. However, it is essential that Aboriginal people learn, or relearn, traditional knowledge to contribute to the healing of Mother Earth. The traditional knowledge and voices of Aboriginal peoples must be acknowledged and heard. Let us make the future of education for our children an even grander story—with the revival and reinforcement of our own ways of learning and seeing the world. One of the most important aspects of Aboriginal learning is our oral traditions; Aboriginal people the world over use the oral traditions in their learning. It is imperative that this transmission of the knowledge, culture and wisdom be a central and vital part of the 21st century. Let our story continue, as it has for so many generations before us. . . .

APPENDIX: QUESTIONS FOR INTERVIEWS ON ABORIGINAL EPISTEMOLOGY AND PEDAGOGY

- If at any time you feel uncomfortable during the interview, let me know.
- Do you mind if I record this interview?
- Who are you? That is, who is your family?
- How did Aboriginal people come to know about plants?
- What do they know about plants? How much of the knowledge remains?
- What do you know about plants?
- How much of the knowledge you possess about plants and medicines is common knowledge?
- Can you comment on the sacred knowledge of the medicine lodge?
- Do you think it would be useful to include traditional environmental knowledge in the classroom?
- How do you think it should be done?
- In regards to protocol, what is the best way approach Elders?
- Do you remember how you came to know about this knowledge?
- Tell me some of your stories.

BIBLIOGRAPHY

Aitken, Larry P., and Edwin W. Haler. (1990). *Two Cultures Meet: Pathways for American Indians to Medicine.* Duluth, Minnesota: University of Minnesota.

Burger, Julian. (1990). *The GAIA Atlas of First Peoples.* New York: Anchor Books.

Caduto, Michael, and Joseph Bruchac. (1994). *Keepers of the Night.* Saskatoon, Saskatchewan: Fifth House Publishers.

Caduto, Michael and Joseph Bruchac. (1991a). *Keepers of the Animals.* Saskatoon, Saskatchewan: Fifth House Publishers.

Caduto, Michael and Joseph Bruchac. (1991b). *Keepers of the Earth*. Saskatoon, Saskatchewan: Fifth House Publishers.

Cajete, Gregory. (1994). *Look to the Mountain: An Ecology of Indigenous Education*. Durango, Colorado: Kivaki Press.

Chomsky, Noam. (1993). *Year 501: The Conquest Continues*. Montreal: Black Rose Books.

Deloria, Vine Jr. (1991). *Indian Education in America*. Boulder, Colorado: American Indian science and engineering society.

Draft Declaration of Indigenous Rights. (1993). Annex 1.

Ermine, Willie. (1995). "Aboriginal Epistemology." In Marie Battiste and Jean Barman, eds., *First Nations Education in Canada: The Circle Unfolds*, pp. 101–112. Vancouver: UBC Press.

Hampton, Eber. (1995). "Towards a Re-definition of American Indian Education." In Marie Battiste and Jean Barman, eds., *First Nations education in Canada: The Circle Unfolds*, pp. 5–46. Vancouver: UBC Press.

Hart, E. P. (1987). *Study for Saskatchewan Schools: Field Study Report*. SIDU research project #6. Regina: Faculty of Education, University of Saskatchewan.

Inter Press Service. (1993). *Story Earth: Native Voices on the Environment*. San Francisco: Mercury House.

Johnson, Martha. (1992). *Lore: Capturing Traditional Environmental Knowledge*. Hay River: Dene Cultural Institute.

Katz, Richard, and Verna St. Denis. (1991). "Teacher as Healer." *Journal of Indigenous Studies* 2: 23–26.

McIvor, Madeline. (1995). "Redefining Science Education for Aboriginal Students." In Marie Battiste and Jean Barman, eds., *First Nations Education in Canada: The Circle Unfolds*, pp. 73–100. Vancouver: UBC Press.

Milne, Sally. (n.d.). "Teachings of the Elder. Why?" Unpublished.

Ogawa, Masakata. (1986). "Toward a New Rationale of Science Education in a Non-Western Society." *European Journal of Science Education* 8: 113–119.

Pomeroy, Debra. (1994). "Science Education and Cultural Diversity: Mapping the Field." Paper to be published in *Science Education*.

Pomeroy, Deborah. (1992). "Science across Cultures: Building Bridges between Traditional Western and Alaskan Native Sciences." *The History and Philosophy of Science in Science Education* 11: 257–267.

Saskatchewan Education. (1990). *Science: A Curriculum Guide for the Elementary Level*. Regina: Saskatchewan Education.

Suzuki, David, and Peter Knudtson. (1992). *Wisdom of the Elders*. New York: Bantam Books.

Vontabel, Roy. (1989). "Two Ways of Knowing." *Caribou news* 9: 2.

wa'Thiongo, Ngugi. (1986). *Decolonizing the Mind: The Politics of Language in African Literature*. London: James Currey.

Wolfe, Alexander. (1988). *Earth Elder Stories*. Saskatoon, Saskatchewan: Fifth House.

Wolfson, Evelyn. (1993). *From the Earth to Beyond the Sky*. Boston: Houghton Miffin Company.

Northern Education Task Force (1989). *Report to the Minister of Education: Summary of Findings*. Regina: Saskatchewan Education.

Indian and Metis Education Advisory Committee Report (1992). *Developments in Indian and Metis Education (1991–1992)*. Regina: Saskatchewan Education.

Studies in Science Education, 1994

Science Curriculum Guide for the Elementary Level, 1990

PLANT RESOURCES

Anderson, Anne. (n.d.). *Some Native Herbal Remedies*.

Assiniwi, Bernard. (1972). *Survival in the Bush*. Toronto: Copp Clark Publishing Company.

Brown-Erichsen, Charlotte. (1979). *Medicinal and Other Uses of North American Plants*. New York: Dover Publications, Inc.

Caduto, Michael, and Joseph Bruchac. (1994). *Keepers of Life*. Saskatoon, Saskatchewan: Fifth House Publishers.

Carmichael, Lloyd T. (1966). *Woodland Wildflowers of Eastern Saskatchewan*. Regina, Saskatchewan: Department of Natural Resources.

Carmichael, Lloyd T. (1967). *Saskatchewan Wildflowers*. Regina, Saskatchewan: Department of Natural Resources.

Densmore, Frances. (1928). *How Indians Use Wild Plants for Food, Medicine and Crafts*. New York: Dover Publications, Inc.

Hutchens, Alma R. (1992). *A Handbook of Native American Herbs*. Boston & London: Shambhala.

Hutchens, Alma R. (1971). *Indian Herbalogy of North America*. Boston & London: Shambhala.

Jaegar, E. (1987). *Indian Reprints: Wildwood Wisdom*. New York: The Macmillan Company.

Jason, Dan, Nancy Jason and Linda Gilbert. (1975). *Some Useful Wild Plants*. Vancouver: Talon Books.

Keanne, Kahlee [Root Woman]. (1994). *Native Medicines*. Saskatchewan: Root Woman and Dave.

Keanne, Kahlee [Root Woman]. (1993). *More Useful Wild Plants of Saskatchewan. Book 2*. Saskatchewan: Root Woman and Dave.

Keanne, Kahlee [Root Woman]. (1992). *Useful Wild Plants of Saskatchewan. Book 1*. Saskatchewan: Root Woman and Dave.

Leighton, Anna. (1986). *A Guide to 20 Plants and Their Uses by the Cree*. La Ronge: Education Branch of the Lac La Ronge Indian Band.

Neithammer, Carolyn. (1974). *American Indian Food and Lore*. New York: Collier Books.

Rowe, J. S., and L. M. Teed. (n.d.). *Saskatchewan Trees*. Saskatoon, Saskatchewan: Tri-Leaf Publications.

Saskatchewan Environmental Resources Management. (1993). *Guide to Forest Understory Vegetation in Saskatchewan*.

Shay, C. Thomas. (1984). "Plants and People: Past Ethnobotany of the Northeastern Prairie." *The Prairie: Past, Present, and Future. Proceedings of the ninth North American Prairie Conference*, July/August, Minnesota.

TREEmendous Saskatchewan Foundation Inc. (1992). *TREEmendous Trees and Shrubs.*

Vance, F. R., J. R. Jowsey and J. S. McLean. (1977). *Wildflowers across the Prairies.* Saskatoon: Western Producer Prairie Books.

Weiner, Michael. (1972). *Earth Medicines—Earth Foods.* New York: Collier-Macmillan Publishers.

AUDIO TAPES

Nerburn, Kent and Louise Mengelkoch (eds.). (1993). *Native American Wisdom.* California: New World Library. (audio tape)

RESOURCE PEOPLE

Keanne, Kahlee [Root Woman]. Saskatoon, Saskatchewan.

Milne, Sally. Lac La Ronge Indian Band. La Ronge, Saskatchewan.

Wilson, Vicki. Elder, Wonska Cultural School. Prince Albert, Saskatchewan.

Modelling: An Aboriginal Approach

Ida Swan

Introduction

In the northern communities of Saskatchewan, as in any geographical area where Indian children are taught, the educators, non-Aboriginal and Aboriginal, must change their instructional methods to accommodate the Aboriginal teaching styles of the communities. The educators must become active learners of the traditional teaching patterns so they can enhance the quality of education that they transmit to the children (Gilliland, 1992; Brown, 1979; Battiste, unpublished). Furthermore, teachers would do well to recognize that nature has always been the best teacher in northern areas of Canada. It was the varied experiences in the natural world that enabled the northern Aboriginal people to use modelling as a fundamental approach; to formulate understandings of the land and to develop the ability to predict to a high degree (Ross, 1992). The animals, plants, waters and the sky participated in teaching the people how to read signs accurately as a means of survival. Although it may not be totally relevant to learn exactly the same skills that were required in years past to survive in the natural world, the modelling approach remains relevant for teaching skills that are essential for the personal and professional growth of Aboriginal children. Teachers must be cognizant of the fact that, in teaching Aboriginal children, the educational process extends beyond the act of transmitting book learnings of ideas and concepts that are foreign and out of the cultural context of the children. The modelling approach is culturally relevant and would be in keeping with traditional Aboriginal perspectives.

The process of modelling is reality-oriented and involves every aspect of Aboriginal culture. It is the means of understanding anything and everything on Earth that affects the people. It creates a sense of connectedness with the physical, mental, psychological and spiritual world of the Northern Cree. Rupert Ross (*Dancing with a Ghost*, 1992) writes that the Ojibway of Ontario embraced these same ideas and understandings

on modelling as did the Cree. The modelling approach contains appropriate
themes that correlate with the Aboriginal traditional and contemporary
lifestyles. It coincides with the current and future needs of students.

This paper will examine literature that advocates the quest for an
Aboriginal idea and approach that can be utilized in the teaching of
Aboriginal students at any level. Secondly, this paper will also propose the
modelling approach as a foundation in the education of Aboriginal
children. The author believes that the modelling approach is applicable to
the learning styles of children in any geographical region of Canada.

EMPOWERMENT, INTERACTION AND DECOLONIZATION

Cummins (1986), Deloria (1991) and Hampton (1995) have advocated
that instructional approaches must begin to incorporate Aboriginal
perspectives to accommodate the cultural learning styles of Indian children.
Cummins (1986) claims that empowering students by permitting them to
become active participants in their own education is essential for success.
He advocates an interactive-participatory learning process that would
enable students to take ownership of their own learnings, increasing the
probability of establishing a connection between life at home and at school.
An interactive-participatory approach would eliminate the present-day
situation where students believe and feel that home and school are separate
entities: currently the home and school environments are perceived as
being responsible for different aspects of human development. As a result,
there is a distinct line between the contributions made by parents and
teachers, negating the value of home experiences in the overall
development of the child. New initiatives must be undertaken to ensure that
valuation is attributed to Aboriginal knowledge.

Deloria (1991), in addressing college students, advised them that the
knowledge they learned from their clans and kinship groups is a valuable
resource that can assist them in their pursuit of academic education
(Deloria, 1991, p. 18). He encourages students to make use of their tribal
knowledge to add meaning to scientific studies, thus removing the cold,
calculating "objective" approach of Western science. The use of tribal
knowledge would lessen the colonizing impact of new ideas and concepts
inherent in scientific studies.

Hampton (1995) sees a need for educators to understand the colonizing impact that instruction based on Western paradigms has on students' attitudes and values and to recognize that the concepts and structures currently practised are foreign to Aboriginal children. For the school to become a place of real learning, emphasizing personal growth rather than professional growth, teachers must accept that the colonizing approaches, concepts and ideas must be removed from the curricula. As Hampton (1995) points out, teachers who understand that the structure and subject matter "subverts the student's self-concept and culture" are more able to facilitate the learnings of Indian children. That is, students would be better off with teachers who recognize that they perpetuate the system because recognition can lead to changes. If educators recognize that the educational system as it exists today negates the child's existence, they can become active participants in changing the educational scene by reflecting on the curricula and its approaches. Such educators can recommend appropriate modes of learning relevant to the area and culture they are teaching, remembering the diversity of all cultures.

Cummins (1986), Deloria (1991) and Hampton (1995) aptly point out that there is a need to make changes in the whole realm of Indian education for Indian children. The changes empower students by including tribal knowledge as a tool to understanding the concepts and ideas being used in school. Furthermore, a decolonizing process must occur with the staff, parents and students to provide an environment that is "caring, thoughtful and purposeful" (Saskatchewan Education, 1992). Maybe then, "The School will recognize that the meaningful involvement of parents, guardians, and community is essential" (Saskatchewan Education, 1992).

EDUCATION: A COMMUNITY RESPONSIBILITY

In every aspect of traditional Aboriginal life, children were involved in the life of the community. They participated in the daily routines of everyday tasks alongside adults who provided guidance through experience rather than by verbal instructions. The learnings that occurred were provided by all members of the kinship group. Grandparents, aunts, uncles and cousins all helped to instill values into the children. There were many occasions for children to watch and learn the knowledge, skills and values of their culture (Hampton, 1995).

Through observation, participation, experience and practice children learned the skills, beliefs, values and norms of their culture, including the understanding that other life processes in the natural world were essential to their survival. Readiness for undertaking a task was not influenced by external forces of coercion. It was up to each person to prepare himself or herself and decide when to accept responsibility. The task of the cultural group was to provide every child with the opportunity to glean as many experiences as were necessary to develop the child into a contributing individual of the community. Thus, each member was given ample time to emulate the duties, behaviours and practices of role models (Hampton, 1995).

Each day was an opportunity for children to develop and become as skilled and knowledgeable as their role models. There was never any doubt that each person would be provided with the opportunity to establish a key role and place within the culture. In all cases, students were taught that all beings of the natural and supernatural world were the most important role models in learning about existence.

A PRIMARY ROLE MODEL

Upon reflecting on the art of modelling, it is extremely difficult to see the connection between what people do, or what people know, versus what is natural. At first glance, modelling seems to be a simple approach requiring no more than the duplication of a representation of an idea, skill or concept, or copying the actions of another individual. Granted, this may be true with young children as they learn from their mothers and fathers to perform simple household chores: hauling water, sweeping the floor, fixing simple things or being in charge of running the motor boat. These skills are essential to the personal development of the individual. All people must learn to do simple things before they can develop the ability to learn more complicated skills.

The approach to modelling that Rupert Ross discusses is comprehensive and complex. He writes that the "the ability to make accurate predictions" develops over a long period of time, culminating in the "capacity for thinking in terms of pattern correspondence" (Ross, 1992, p. 78). It is a complex, developmental process that requires the individual to be totally immersed in the natural environment. The learnings of the natural world are possible when individuals become totally aware of their immediate surroundings: to see, hear, feel and absorb all the movements and patterns in nature. Indeed, the individual must become a part of the totality of the world. The complete physical, emotional, mental and spiritual involvement is necessary to facilitate the full meaning of the stimuli and to be able to use these stimuli to one's advantage.

In traditional societies, when things, occurrences and events in nature were observed, the Aboriginal hunter-gatherer absorbed the messages and was able to predict weather patterns and/or animal behaviours. Thus, based on knowledge obtained from nature, hunting/gathering activities reflected the messages ascertained from the natural world. For example, if the beaver lodges were built high above the water level, the hunter knew it was going to be a long winter. The knowledge from messages obtained from nature would precipitate activities focused on making preparations for a long, cold winter. Even in today's world, fishermen will check the sky before they go out on the lake, knowing full well that a sudden storm can be very dangerous. Fishermen and other people who spend a lot of time on the big lakes have the ability to manoeuvre a boat on rough waters. Somehow, they use the weight of the boat and the direction of the wind to prevent themselves from capsizing.

There is no doubt that Aboriginal people have learned to make use of technological tools to their advantage, but many people are cognizant of the knowledge of the care-giver, knowing that the tool itself cannot provide food. It has to be used within the context of cultural realities. Deloria expands on this idea. He wrote that Aboriginal people "sought to preserve the idea of relationships of the natural world within the technology that arose as a result of our learning experiences" (Deloria, 1991, p. 29). The tool by itself is incapable of providing food. It is useful only when the patterns and movements in nature are observed and understood. It is no wonder that hunting tools are held in high respect. My father, for example, would not allow children to play with guns, pouches or bullets because he was fully aware that if he did not adhere to societal beliefs and values about hunting it could affect his ability to provide for his family.

With respect to the Northern Cree, the harsh climate, which has created the six seasons of winter, break-up, spring, summer, fall and freeze-up, has dictated a particular lifestyle. The shaping and moulding of their physical, mental, psychological and spiritual lives were a result of the natural environment in which they lived. Their behaviours, cultural patterns and language were grounded in their experiences of the world.

Psychologically, the Northern Cree have used humour to its full advantage. The person who can laugh at himself or herself is held in high esteem by his or her peers. Humour and the ability to see humour in events and incidents has kept the Northern Cree from being swallowed by the hardships that they have to endure. It has helped them keep their perspectives, able to respond to the demands of the land, and has allowed them to keep their reverence for the environment.

Every action mirrored their beliefs and values. In preparing for a hunt, the individual would make sure that everything that was needed for the hunt was clean and packed properly. After the hunt, meat, hide and bones had to handled carefully as a tribute to the animal and the Creator for enabling the hunter to obtain food for his family. Likewise, the way that people dressed during the different seasons was a demonstration of the respect that the forces of nature were given by the Aboriginal people. For example, the north wind was a formidable force and it received utmost respect. Young people were taught that it was proper to dress fully during the winter to demonstrate awe and respect for the great north wind. Children learned early that showing disrespect could bring discontent to the land and create undue hardships for the people.

It was very important for children to observe and adhere to the rules of conduct and behaviour. They knew that all things were affected by nature, especially humans, and that they had a moral and spiritual responsibility to follow the patterns of conduct and behaviour for the social good (Ross, 1993). The lives of the Northern Cree were not easy, but they learned to adapt and make life meaningful according to the teachings of nature. Consequently, adult members were very diligent in their roles as perpetuators of the cultural beliefs, values and norms.

MODELLING IN TODAY'S WORLD

Today, the social role that parents and other adults enjoyed within the social organization of previous generations has largely been displaced by the educational system. The school programs and approaches are as responsible for the erosion of cultures as are the churches and the government. Education has removed the valuable role that adults enjoyed within the social fabric of the culture by its structure, especially in the timing of the school year. This has created a loss of cultural role models, resulting in social disharmony and dislocation for families.

The young people are not able to obtain skills and practices from traditional role models due to the structure of the school year and day. The school day absorbs all the daylight hours, disrupting the chores and responsibilities of families. When the parents are tending to chores at home, the children are at school and they miss valuable opportunities to observe and learn traditional and contemporary skills. Fathers are unable to pass on knowledge and skills to their sons, because the trapping season and most of the fishing season do not coincide with the time that school is in progress (Ross, 1992).

As a result, parents, as important participants of the learning process, are made dysfunctional by the educational structures. Since it is the structure of the educational system that has in part contributed to dysfunctions within family systems due to missed learnings that are meaningful to the culture, it should be obligatory for the school to create conditions that can revitalize some of the skills with which the people sustained themselves for thousands of years. Band-controlled schools are also victims of an educational system operated under provincial guidelines, but the obligation to revitalize the cultures falls more heavily on their shoulders. In the words of Hampton, "It is through me no less than anyone else that my people live" (1995, p. 19). It is the responsibility of every Aboriginal to work towards correcting the wrongs that have been inflicted on Aboriginal people.

Aboriginal people and organizations are inherently responsible for the evaluation, analysis and reorganization of the educational system. Those who work within the system must address the real needs of the students instead of concentrating on teaching provincial programs that perpetuate the belief that educational attainment will ensure the obtainment of the "pot of gold" at the end of the rainbow. A few good teachers promoting holistic learning processes is no longer sufficient if the system continues to exist. The whole process and purpose of Aboriginal education must be established at the community level if it is to benefit Aboriginal people.

Traditional pedagogies must be sought to ensure that previous mistakes are not repeated. Pedagogies that reflect the philosophies of the culture must be resurrected and made available to all parties concerned. The pedagogy of modelling needs all members to work together to ensure success. It is a viable method for recognizing the contribution of community members and for re-establishing cultural values about Aboriginal pedagogy.

Traditionally, the responsibilities of the kinship group were an important factor in maintaining and sustaining the culture. This concept can be expanded into the school by giving back the responsibility of teaching and learning to the parents, thereby acknowledging that the educational system is not capable of providing all the knowledge and wisdom that is required to sustain the culture in a changing world that is constantly being bombarded by outside influences: forces that can negate parental and cultural values and are not easy to deal with. For example, cable television and the telephone systems in the north have effectively removed the need for people to visit and exchange ideas.

The idea of modelling can assist in reversing the situation in promoting good programming and exposing students to interactive approaches that enable them to exchange ideas about the impact of outside forces, negative and positive. It is crucial in today's world, more than before, that community and cultural members of the group plan together and revisit their collective experiences, learn from each other and reclaim the sacred trust to the land (Cajete, 1994) and to each other.

Furthermore, opportunities must be created within school programs that promote interaction between the young people and the old people. The cultural program of Pelican Narrows promotes the involvement of elders as teachers and transmitters of knowledge. This is a good beginning, but cultural experiences and elder interactions must be expanded to the rest of the school to make it truly a part of the learnings of every student. Ownership cannot be given totally to the cultural programs in promoting traditional and contemporary perspectives on teaching and learning.

Deloria (1989) claims that the concept of kinship and clan relations is rooted in the idea that every individual is responsible to every other member in the group to ensure that correct behaviour is adhered to; thus, the values, norms and beliefs are perpetuated by everyone. It is up to each and every member to accept the responsibility of proper conduct so that the "society as whole would function" (Deloria, 1989, p. 21). Therefore, ownership of teaching must include the community from which the ideas and concepts are taken. It becomes vital to teach the approach of modelling to learn the correct way of doing things. Through repeated experiences and associations with adults in the community, other forgotten modes of transmitting knowledge, like using subtle signs of communication, can be learned by the students. Re-establishing traditional modes of transmitting knowledge can rebuild the social fabric of the community.

CONCLUSION

Applying the pedagogy of modelling in the school and community could lead to a greater understanding of the role that teachers, students and community members have within the whole area of Aboriginal education for Aboriginal children. There is much work to be done in the area of colonization, but some aspects of modelling can be utilized even within the current system. The key point to remember is that the complex aspect of modelling as it pertains to Aboriginal understandings of the real and natural world can only be fully understood by associating with people who are still very much a part of their environment.

Swisher and Deyhle (1992) have expressed the need for educators to learn the social traditions, norms, values and patterns of each community. Aboriginal teachers who are well grounded in their cultural roots sometimes forget their qualities and fail to use them to enhance the personal growth of their students. They must be encouraged to use their abilities to recognize the unique behaviours and teaching styles of their cultures. Non-Aboriginal educators would benefit from learning the Aboriginal modelling approach from community members and apply it, in and out of their classrooms. This would enable educators to meet the needs of the students and ensure success. By using the modelling approach, students would be empowered with the skills to adjust to social, cultural and economic changes, and still maintain the traditional values that have sustained their culture for thousands of years. Students who are well grounded in their traditional values will be more able to ward off the negative attitudes that "society at large" has of First Nations people. With a good grounding in their cultures and understanding of tribal knowledge of the natural world, they can adjust to any situation. The complex approach of modelling is an approach and a process that will enable students to realize that adjustment is as much a part of the mind as the physical aspect of human existence.

REFERENCES

Battiste, M.A. (n.d.) "You Can't Be the Doctor, if You're the Disease: The Tenets of Systematic Colonialism in Canada." Unpublished manuscript, INEP, University of Saskatchewan.

Brown, Anthony D. (1979). "Cross-over Effect: A Legitimate Issue in Indian Education." In *Multicultural Education and the American Indian*, pp. 93–107. Contemporary American Indian series, no. 2.

Cajete, G. (1994). *Look to the Mountain: An Ecology of Indigenous Education*. Durango, Colorado: Kivaki Press.

Cummins, Jim (1986). "Empowering Indian Students: What Teachers and Parents Can Do." In Jon Reyhner, ed., *Teaching American Indian Students*, pp. 3–12. Norman and London: University of Oklahoma Press, 1992.

Deloria, Vine, Jr. (1991). *Indian Education in America*. Boulder, Colorado.

Gilliland, Hap. (1992). *Teaching the Native American*. 2nd ed. Dubuque, Iowa: Kendall/ Hunt Publishing Company.

Hampton, Eber. (1995). "Towards a Re-definition of American Indian Education." In Marie Battiste and Jean Barman, eds., *First Nations Education in Canada: The Circle Unfolds*, pp. 5–46. Vancouver: UBC Press.

Ross, Rupert. (1992). *Dancing with a Ghost: Exploring Indian Reality*. Markham, Ontario: Reed Books.

Saskatchewan Education, Training, and Employment. (1994). *Policy Directions for Secondary Education in Saskatchewan: Minister's Response to the High School Review Advisory Committee Final Report*. Saskatchewan Education.

Swisher, Karen, and Donna Deyhle. (1992). "Adapting Instruction to Culture." In Jon Reyhner, ed., *Teaching American Indian Students*, pp. 81–95. Norman and London: University of Oklahoma Press.

ABORIGINAL PEDAGOGY: THE SACRED CIRCLE CONCEPT

ANGELINA WEENIE

As an Aboriginal educator, it is apparent to me that the resistance and alienation of Aboriginal students is escalating. It is also evident that fragmented Aboriginal knowledge systems contribute to a problem-ridden education system. To address these issues, we are compelled to seek out traditional teachings and find a new understanding of Aboriginal pedagogy.

Our education system is dominated by the Western world-view, which is "an atomistic view of the universe in which reality is seen to consist of separate, isolated building blocks" (Miller, Cassie and Drake, 1990, p. 3). The interconnections between subjects are not made and fragmentation becomes the main problem facing educators (Miller et al., 1990, p. 2). In the Aboriginal world-view, the learning process is viewed holistically. The learning process is described as "a process of internalization and actualization within oneself in a total way" (Lightning, 1992, p. 243). It is this philosophy that informs our approach to teaching.

The holistic approach to attaining knowledge encompasses four domains—mental, physical, emotional and spiritual. Aboriginal epistemology or Aboriginal ways of knowing centre on spirituality. In the Aboriginal world-view, "the spirit and the heart are essential ways of knowing" (Katz and St. Denis, 1991, p. 31). Language and culture are "crucial components in the transformative learning process" (Ermine, 1995, p. 102). Prayer and ceremony are also "instruments in Aboriginal ways of knowing" (Ermine, 1995, p. 109). Education in the Cree way of life is seen as "a life long quest which require[s] patience, introspection, mistakes, sacrifices and spirituality" (Fiddler and Sanderson, 1991, n.p.).

The challenges in First Nations education can be met by revitalizing Aboriginal epistemology and by introducing "a philosophy of educating for balance, harmony and well-being for the human condition" (Lightning, 1992, p. 253). Katz and St. Denis state that "teaching must welcome back the healing dimension" (1991, p. 25), and this concept of teaching as healing redefines the role of the teacher. The "teacher as healer" fosters the connections between the student, the community and the culture and is "one who seeks to make things whole" (Katz and St. Denis, 1991, p. 24).

Healing is defined as "a transitioning toward meaning, balance, connectedness and wholeness" (Katz and St. Denis, 1991, p. 24). Focusing on the self begins the process of healing. Ermine states that, "Ultimately, it was in the self that Aboriginal people discovered great resources for coming to grips with life's mysteries" (1995, p. 108). Seeking out inner guidance through "subjective experiences and introspection" (Ermine, 1995, p. 102) is the first step. This introspection can be attained through ceremonies, such as sweat lodges, fasting and sun dances.

The change process also requires the development of critical consciousness that will lead "to the humane transformation of, rather than a passive accommodation to one's world" (McLaren, 1989, p. 235). In critical theory, classroom pedagogical approaches centre on student experiences or cultures. Cummins maintains that "pedagogical approaches that empower students encourage them to assume greater control over setting their own learning goals" (1988, p. 312). The primary orientation of Indigenous teaching and learning, which is that "each person is their own teacher" (Cajete, 1994, p. 227), needs to be utilized.

The sacred circle or medicine wheel concept is "part of the critical theory of education committed to human emancipation" (Regnier, 1994, p. 129). The sacred circle or medicine wheel is a traditional symbolic circle. A medicine wheel is defined "as a prominent, centrally located stone cairn of stone . . . of varying size from the centre of which radiate a series of rows of other stones or the margins of a stone ring" (Fiddler and Sanderson, 1991, n.p.). It was used to mark the grave of a chief. It also symbolizes the Aboriginal world-view of "connecting the physical world with the metaphysical" (Fiddler and Sanderson, 1991, n.p.).

The medicine wheel is "a model which can be used to examine our lives holistically and deepen the meaning of our journey. The essence of the wheel is movement and change" (Fiddler and Sanderson, 1991, n.p.). Learning, teaching and human development are viewed as a process, and the medicine wheel can be used as a philosophical framework for developing healing pedagogy.

Regnier (1994) describes how the sacred circle concept is used as a process pedagogy of healing at Joe Duquette High School in Saskatoon, Saskatchewan. The three phases of process pedagogy as healing are belonging, understanding and critical reflection. The circle is used as "a first step to overcoming isolation, self-denial, exclusion, being disenfranchised, alienation, and loss of identity" (Regnier, 1994, p. 138).

By using the circle, the teacher can make the classroom a healing community. Story circles and drama are other ways of drawing on students' experiences and making meaning of them. Journal writing is part of reflection. Another teaching strategy around the Aboriginal learners' world-view is the whole language approach. This strategy "aims to liberate students . . . and encourage[s] them to become active generations of their own knowledge" (Cummins, 1988, p. 7).

You have
noticed that everything an
Indian does is in a circle, and that is because
the Power of the World always works in circles, and
everything tries to be round. In the old days when we were a
strong and happy people all our power came to us from the sacred
hoop of the nation and so long as the hoop was unbroken the people flourished.
The flowering tree was the living centre of the hoop and the circle of the four
quarters nourished it. The East gave peace and light, the South gave warmth, the
West gave rain and the North, with its cold and mighty wind, gave strength and
endurance. This knowledge came to us from the outerworld with our religion. Everything the Power of the World does is done in a circle. The sky is round and I have
heard that the earth is round like a ball and so are all the stars. The Wind, in its
greatest power, whirls. Birds make their nests in circles, for theirs is the same
religion as ours. The Sun comes forth and goes down again in circle. The
Moon does the same and both are round. Even the seasons form a great circle
in their changing and always come back again to where they were.
The life of a man is a circle, from childhood to childhood and so it is
in everything where power moves. Our tipis were round
like the nests of birds and these were always set in a circle,
the nation's hoop, a nest of many nests, where the
Great Spirit meant for us to hatch
our Children.

[*Black Elk Speaks*, as told through John G. Neihardt (Lincoln: University of Nebraska Press, 1961)]

Gilliland and Reyhner (1988) use the medicine wheel as metaphor to inspire creative writing. East symbolizes the creative spirit, south represents emotions, west is the place of intuition and north represents wisdom. Gilliland and Reyhner explain that we can "start with emotions in the South. We connect these with our minds and inner wisdom of the North. Our creative spirit is connected with our bodies which hold all memory. In the centre is the mystery which we allow to happen in creativity, blending all of the elements" (Gilliland and Reyhner, 1988, 130).

The foundation for teaching and learning is in Indigenous cultures. Life and learning is a process and in our search for knowledge we begin to have an understanding of humility and compassion. Kisewatisowin, which refers to "the sacredness of all relationship" (Fiddler and Sanderson, 1991, n.p.), is the most important teaching we are to carry with us. *Kisewatisowin*, or the attainment of compassionate mind, will help us achieve balance and harmony (Lightning, 1992, p. 218).

In summary, then, the main principle of Aboriginal pedagogy is respect for knowledge, for the student, for the community and for the culture. Aboriginal pedagogy is nurturing to bring out knowledge. Let us remember Cajete's words: that "Indigenous teaching is planted like a seed, then nurtured and cultivated through the relationship of teacher and student until it bears fruit" (Cajete, 1994, p. 223).

APPENDIX: MODELS

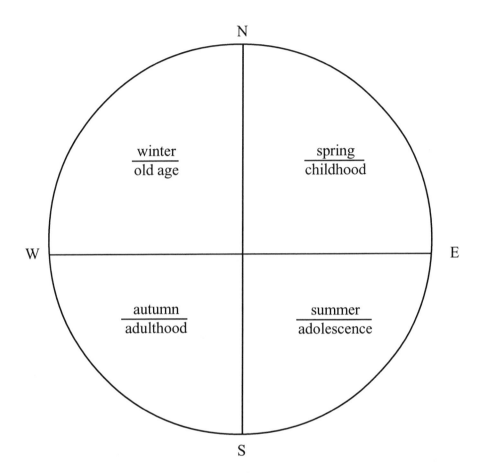

1. Circle of life—*Nehiyaw Pimatisowin*

The Sacred Circle represents the Aboriginal world-view: "it symbolizes harmony and the belief that life occurs within a series of circular movements that govern their relationship with the environment" (Regnier, 1994, p. 129).

This symbol can be used to understand seasons, directions, stages of life and the elements.

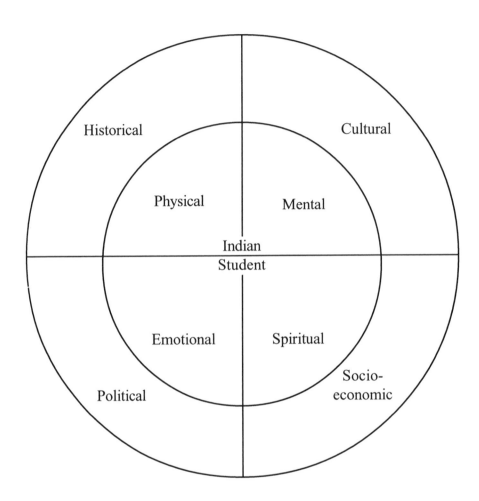

2. The forces that shape a child

Unless a child learns about the forces that shape him, the history of his people, their values and customs, their language, he will never really know himself or his potential as a human being (National Indian Brotherhood, 1972).

Source: Rita Bouvier, Saskatchewan Teachers Federation, and Verna St. Denis, Indian Teacher Education Program

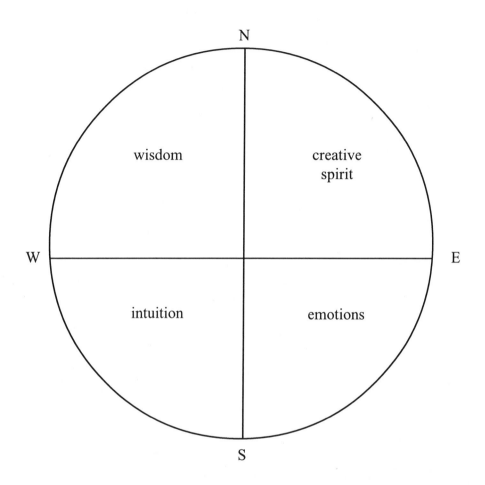

3. Use of the medicine wheel to inspire creative writing
"The East is symbolic of the sun and fire and our own creative spirit. The South represents water and our emotions. The West is the place of Mother Earth and our intuition; the place of magic and dreams. North represents air and our minds filled with wisdom as we learn about the mystery of life" (Gilliland and Reyhner, 1988, p. 130).

REFERENCES

Black Elk Speaks. (1961). As told through John G. Neihardt. Lincoln: University of Nebraska Press.

Cajete, G. (1994). *Look to the Mountain. An Ecology of Indigenous Education*. Durango, Colorado: Kivaki Press.

Cummins, J. (1988). "Empowering Indian Students: What Teachers and Parents Can Do." In J. Reyhner, ed., *Teaching the Indian Child: A Bilingual/Multicultural Approach*, pp. 301–317. Billings, Montana: Eastern Montana College.

Ermine, Willie (1995). "Aboriginal Epistemology." In Marie Battiste and Jean Barman, eds., *The Circle Unfolds*, pp. 101–112. Vancouver: UBC Press.

Fiddler, S., and J. Sanderson. (1991). *Medicine Wheel Concept from the World View of the Plains and Parkland Cree Culture*. Regina, Saskatchewan: Saskatchewan Indian Federated College.

Gilliland, H., and J. Reyhner. (1988). *Teaching the Native American*. Iowa: Kendall/Hunt Publishing Company.

Katz, R., and V. St. Denis. (1991). "Teacher as Healer." *Journal of Indigenous Studies* 2: 24–36.

Lightning, W. (1992). "Compassionate Mind: Implications of a Text Written by Elder Louis Sunchild." *Canadian Journal of Native Education* 19: 215–253.

McLaren, P. (1989). *Life in Schools: An Introduction to Critical Pedagogy in the Foundations of Education*. Toronto: Irwin Publishing.

Miller, J. P., J. R. B. Cassie and S. M. Drake. (1990). *Holistic Learning: A Teacher's Guide to Integrated Studies*. Toronto: Ontario Institute for Studies in Education.

National Indian Brotherhood. (1972).

Regnier, R. (1994). "The Sacred Circle: A Process Pedagogy of Healing." *Interchange* 25 (12): 129–144.

TRADITIONAL PARENTING

JANE HARP

Children of First Nations are special gifts from the Creator. Their
lives and thoughts have special meaning and significance and they
are to be treated with care, love and respect. Children of First
Nations have a right to understand and interact with the world in
their own First Nations' language, to be nurtured by their parents,
grandparents, and communities and to the teaching and guidance of
their Elders. [FSIN, 1990]

Historically, the laws of First Nations were clear about the welfare of
their children because they knew that the futures of their nations were
directly related to the well-being of their children. Parents were the first
line of responsibility. In the past, parenting among Indian people was not
left to chance. Well-defined customs, values and practices were handed
down from generation to generation. Through these practices, parents, an
extended family member or an interested citizen of the community would
assume responsibility for the child. However, these ancestral ways were not
to last. With the coming of the white man, this way of life would
dramatically change.

The changes and breakdown of the First Nations families began with
the colonization and the assimilation policies of the federal government,
which were legalized through the Indian Act of 1876. The First Nations
family was fractured and weakened. The residential school era consisted of
removing children from parental control, which proved devastating to the
First Nations family system. The residential schools systematically
discouraged and ridiculed Native languages and practices associated with
native culture (McKenzie and Hudson, 1988).

It has been said that one of the consequences of this alienation of
children from their families is that the traditional parenting role was not
handed down to the next generation. It may account for many of the
problems related to child care that are prevalent among Native parents

(McKenzie and Hudson, 1988). Some of the effects of the residential school education system also include the loss of the Native language, which is a vital link to the Native culture. Loss of identity became acute. Psychologically, Native children learned fear, self-hate, humiliation, shame and anger. This suffering manifests itself throughout the First Nations and has a direct impact on alcohol and drug use, suicides, tragic deaths and the general disarray of communities (First Nations Child and Family Task Force, 1993).

Similarly, the provincial child welfare systems have been involved in the separation of Native children from their families, communities and culture. Native children are placed in white foster homes where they are faced with a totally different environment and culture. Recent 1994 provincial statistics figures indicate that there are 1,258 Native children in foster care in the Prince Albert district alone. The child welfare system paid little attention to the ways in which Native communities traditionally handled parental neglect or child care problems through communal and serial patterns of parenting.

Some of these Native children have known no other home and are totally alienated from their families and culture. McKenzie and Hudson (1988) stated that transmission of knowledge and patterns of child care were greatly interrupted, and re-establishment of these have proved very different for Native communities.

It is true that Aboriginal people cannot recapture the past as it once was. However, we can still find great value in our child-rearing traditions. Incorporation of traditional child-rearing practices can only enhance our experience as modern-day parents.

Many bands believed that children were special gifts from the Creator. Elders encourage positive and loving relationships between parents and their children. This is usually done by using praise and reassurance. Some of the child-rearing practices consist of prophecies being made about the worth of a child and his/her future. The child's growth and development are recognized through rite-of-passage ceremonies. These ceremonies are important to the child as well. In particular, the naming ceremony helps a child establish his or her identity in the tribe or band.

Tribes and bands usually consist of small communities of people. The children quickly learn to share and to show respect for elders. Everyone knows the consequence of breaking the community's rules or limits. Discipline is carefully thought out to fit a child's need to understand a specific rule or limit.

Nurturance forms an important part of traditional child-rearing. Cradleboards mean that infants are rarely separated from their mothers. Extended family members such as the grandparents, aunts, uncles and cousins play a major role and are always nearby to help parents with their responsibilities in raising their families. Some extended family members have specific roles such as the grandfather being the storyteller and the uncle being the disciplinarian.

Storytelling and legends are also a large part of traditional child-rearing. These stories and legends enable the children to learn about proper relationships with other people and the environment. Children become good listeners and regard the words as sacred. Children also learn to be good observers and understand the meaning of non-verbal communication.

The old ways provide important elements of positive parenting. Children brought up in the old ways are respected and understood by the traditional people. Relationships between child and parent are important, and communication is well developed. Moral development receives constant and careful attention. Although living in a more complex world today, our ancestors provide strong models of child-rearing practices for Indian parenting today (Northwest Indian Child Welfare Institute, 1986)

CREE AND OJIBWAY PARENTING

It is common knowledge that many Aboriginal people share various values and world-views. It is a fact also that there are many First Nations in Canada, each with its own child-rearing patterns, value systems, communications patterns and behaviors.

CREE CHILD-REARING

Traditionally, the Cree children internalized their cultural values and beliefs during the first five or six years of their lives. The child learned the Cree language, internalized traditional cognitive patterns of thought, norms and expectations about how to behave, and began to practise skills appropriate for his or her age and sex. Among the Cree, there was a long process of apprenticeship that was begun under a parent as well as older siblings. Instruction was given by example with little direct explanation or guidance. Learning self-reliance, each child had to learn to do things for himself with minimal help from others (Chance, 1968). It was also important that children learn quickly to co-operate and share with others; everyone understood the boundaries set by their community's rules. Discipline was meted out to fit the need for the child to understand the rule. Punishment for fighting or other mischief was mild, usually involving teasing, laughter or ridicule, reinforced by threats of possible supernatural sanctions. The legend of Wihtiko was commonly used to keep a child in line. Wihtiko was believed by the Cree to be an entity or entities with great powers who could do unbelievable things with their medicine. These powerful people could cure you, or they could make you really sick by calling on their spirit friends to do things for them. The legend is that, in the cold months of winter, when food was scarce, some of these powerful people would turn into a Wihtiko. This being would eat its family and friends in the camp and then wander, looking for more people to eat.

Nurturance played an important part in the Cree child-rearing practices. Cree mothers tended to have more than 10 children and would breastfeed all of them. As one Cree mother related, "God has given us breasts with which to give life to our children" (Ahenakew, 1992). Breastfeeding greatly enhanced bonding between the mother and her child. Breastfeeding tended to continue till the child was a toddler. At birth, the child was swaddled in a mossbag, which provided a sense of security and safety. Indian midwives were commonly used in Cree communities. These services were usually performed by an aunt, grandmother or female neighbour.

Moral development was taught by relating legends or stories that had moral points or significance to it. The Cree trickster, Weesakayjac, was commonly used for this purpose. In addition, to encourage doing household chores, children or young teens were told that dishes left unwashed would get done by the devil. Children were also told that watching animals, especially dogs, copulate, would result in blindness. Another story, close to home, was that sewing on a Sunday would prick the body of God or some other deity. Respect for elders and parents was strongly emphasized. Children valued the advice and guidance that was freely given by their parents, grandparents and other extended family members, as well as other respected community members.

OJIBWAY CHILD-REARING

The Ojibway people were very resilient and, like the Cree, had a common linguistic and cultural heritage that had roots in the distant past. In the Ojibway culture, kinship was organized in such a way that the child had many siblings other than his or her own natural ones. For instance, an uncle was considered like a father to the child, and therefore the child's cousins were viewed as his or her siblings. The child had many role models on which to pattern his or her overall development. Hallowell (1992) stated that the term "brother" was perpetuated by male Ojibway children through successive generations.

This pattern of kinship also applied to the women who are "sisters" to his mother. Thus, the socialization process of the Ojibway was multifaceted. The child's growing up was overseen by various relatives. Discipline was administered by his or her uncles, aunts and grandparents.

Anishinabe is another term used to refer to the Ojibway people. The Anishinabe used legends and stories to get their children to behave. For example, a bad spirit on a cold winter night makes the ice on the lake crack as he tries to get out. Children were often told that if they did not stop crying, the bad spirit would get them. Listening to stories taught children to be quiet and pay attention. Ojibway legends and stories often contained events that depicted daily living, feelings, dreams, magic and mystery. Ideas and beliefs were later incorporated, as were religious beliefs, rules and laws and humour. These legends and stories were passed down "from the mouth" to become part of Anishinabe heritage. Storytelling was a sharing process. The people involved in storytelling were important and powerful members of the community. Anishinabe children respected their elders and learned from them. The stories were repeated over and over, with the result that listeners' memories were sharpened (Elston, 1985). Legends compared nature with humanity. These comparisons showed that spirits, nature and humans are all one. With these metaphors or comparisons, the lessons that they meant to teach were easier to remember. The Ojibway people, like other Indian tribes, used the circle for their teaching and learning because it has no beginning and no end.

Like the Cree, the birth of a child was usually attended by a midwife who severed and tied the umbilical cord, dried the child with moss or powdered bison dung, and wrapped it in a piece of soft buckskin or cloth.

Often, the mossbag was fastened to a wooden cradle board. Children were named after an unusual event when they were born, the war exploits of a relative or a distinguishing personal characteristic. Children were nursed from one to five or six years. The entire family lavished affection on small children. As in many cultures, the grandparents doted on their grandchildren. Children were rarely beaten or reprimanded. They were encouraged to become hunters and homemakers by the celebration of the first fruits ceremony. When a boy shot his first deer, or trapped his first bear, his family provided a feast, inviting relatives and neighbours. A similar feast took place when a little girl first brought in firewood or tanned a hide (Higer, 1977).

Like the Cree, the Ojibway had a trickster, called Nanabush, who characterized legends and stories that encompassed lessons and teachings in terms of daily moral, spiritual and well-being of their members.

CONCLUSION

The task of rejuvenating the old ways of child-rearing practices and incorporating them into the modern-day practices will be an arduous one. For generations, the Native people, through their storytelling, elders and other honoured members, have passed along their teachings. These teachings have helped them learn how to survive and exist with one another. Since white contact, Indian people have struggled to hold on to their traditional ways of teaching and learning amidst the dominant society's system of teachers, textbooks and classroom.

Cajete (1994) maintains that, historically, traditional American Indian education occurred in a holistic context. It was an educational process that unfolded through mutual and reciprocal relationships that existed between social groups and the natural world.

Cajete further maintains that this traditional way of Indian education has been lost or eroded by the introduction of the dominant society's perspectives and methods of education. The whole process of Indian education needs to be recreated and reintroduced to the Native people. Cajete states that the key lies in our collective ability to create and to erect a new expression of Indian education in a 21st-century world. Cajete further states that to Indianize the education of Indian people constitutes a major revolution. This is not to say that it is an impossible task, because traditional education evolved from millions of smaller visions that the Indian people individually and collectively consummated. It is our choice how we educate and how we create and realize our visions. The Indian people must choose their own path of learning. Contemporary Western education will have to undergo major transformation to accommodate the re-emergence of traditional Indian education (Cajete, 1994).

There is an emerging theme in child welfare that the Indian people need to rethink and reform their function in the communities with regard to the children. For instance, the Federation of Saskatchewan Indian Nations (FSIN) Child Welfare and Family Support Act (1990) maintains that it is essential, in the creation of culturally appropriate child welfare agencies,

> To identify the precepts, systems, structures, policies and procedures occasioned or confirmed by this Act will be based upon Indian-law; Indian customs and traditions; Indian culture; and Indian standards. [FSIN, 1990]

More and more Indian people have developed or are in the process of setting up their own child welfare agencies. The FSIN has been a forerunner in the development of Indian child care standards, with input from the various tribal councils and First Nations across the province. These Indian child care standards were recognized by the province to be equal or better than its own in July 1992. It is paramount that these Indian child and family services agencies are designed, created, controlled and implemented by Indian people. The types of programs and services will be dictated by the needs of the community. The direction and ownership will come from the community members with the help of the guidance and wisdom of the elders.

The process of reintroducing or rejuvenating the traditional ways of child-rearing practices will involve re-educating Indian parents about the traditional ways of raising their children. This will mean going back to the centre of the circle. There is evidence that more and more Indian people are resuming their Indian spirituality. This has meant a complete healing process for some in terms of redefining their attitudes and values. Embarking on a new way of parenting means experiencing nurturance before one can learn how to nurture. Before parents can learn about their children's needs, they must first learn how to meet their own needs.

Dysfunctional families need to take control of their lives and heal holistically before they can become effective parents and extend the honour, respect, care, protection and nurturance to their children (Northwest Indian Child Welfare Institute, 1986).

Traditionally, children prepared for adulthood by being part of the group and learning the ways of the hunter, warrior, gatherer, caretaker and decision-maker. The environment demanded that they learned their lessons well or their group would not survive. Today, adult roles greatly differ and are influenced by the dangers and challenges of the world today. Today, Indian children must face two cultures whose expectations are not well defined. However, the values about children are as valid today as they were 200 years ago, despite the loss of the old ways of yesteryear. Indian parents are also faced with problems in raising children who have to survive in two worlds. Some Indian parents have also been raised in two cultures. Some parents are traditional, others have completely assimilated into the mainstream society and still others are comfortable with who they are. Some have blended the ways and values of the two cultures. Many Indian parents are confused about their identities. Consequently, they find it hard to give their children a firm sense of identity. By learning their culture holistically and coming to terms with what it means to be Indian, parents can find their own strengths and help their children (Northwest Indian Child Welfare Institute, 1986).

In summary, the focus of this paper has been the discussion of the need to rejuvenate Aboriginal traditional parenting. Traditionally, well-defined customs, values and practices were handed down from generation to generation.

An urgent need exists for Native parents to rediscover how Indian families traditionally taught living and social skills by using nature as a teacher and an ally. The lessons learned from nature taught children how to get along, cope with hardships and find strength. By relearning from nature, Native parents can help their children become strong and at peace with the world (Northwest Indian Child Welfare Institute, 1986). The cyclical journey of the traditional family and group will have to be revisited and revitalized. The roles and responsibilities of the family, extended family, band/community and First Nation will have to undergo redefinition and reaffirmation in terms of validating the importance of traditional parenting in order for our children to become stable and self-confident to carry on the struggle and maintain the survival of an Indian Nation that is holistically healthy in terms of its spiritual, physical, social, emotional and mental well-being. The starting point clearly indicates that we, as Indian people, need to reintroduce ourselves to the coexistence and co-operation of nature and our environment.

REFERENCES

Ahenakew, Fred. (1992). *Our Grandmothers' Lives as Told in Their Own Words.* Saskatoon: Fifth House Publishers.

Cajete, Gregory. (1994). *Look to the Mountain: An Ecology of Indigenous Education.* Durango, Colorado: Kivaki Press.

Chance, Norman A. (1968). *Conflict in Culture: Problems of Developmental Change among the Cree.* Ottawa: Canadian Research Centre for Anthropology, Saint Paul University.

Chance, Norman A. (1959). *Social and Economic Change among the Northern Ojibway.* Toronto: University of Toronto Press.

Charles, Colin. (1984). *The Legend of "Wihtiko."* La Ronge, Saskatchewan: Lac La Ronge Band, Education Branch.

Crowe, Keith J. (1974). *A History of the Original Peoples of Northern Canada.* Montreal: McGill-Queen's University Press.

First Nation's Child and Family Task Force [Manitoba]. (1993). *Children First Our Responsibility.*

Elston, Georgia. 1985. *Ojibway Stories and Legends: From the Children of Curve Lake.* Lakefield: Waapoone Publishing & Promotion.

[FSIN] Federation of Saskatchewan Indian Nations. 1990. *An Act Respecting Indian Nations' Jurisdiction and Control over the Establishment and Delivery of Child Welfare and Family Support Services to Treaty Indian Children and Family.*

Hallowell, A. Irving. 1992. *The Ojibway of Berens River, Manitoba, Ethnography Introduction.* New York: Stanford University, Harcourt Grace J.V. Anovich College Publishers.

Higer, M. Inez. (1977). *Chippewa Child Life and Its Culture Background.* Lincoln, Nebraska: J & L Reprint Company.

Johnston, Basil H. (1981). *Tales the Elders Told: Ojibway Legends.* Toronto: Royal Ontario Museum.

McKenzie, Brad, and Peter Hudson. (1988). *Native Children, Child Welfare and the Colonization of Native People.* Vancouver: University of British Columbia Press.

Northwest Indian Child Welfare Institute, Parry Center for Children. (1986). *Positive Indian Parenting: Honoring Our Children by Honoring Our Traditions, A Model Indian Parent Training Manual.* Portland, Oregon.

A Piece of the Pie: The Inclusion of Aboriginal Pedagogy into the Structures of Public Education

Wally Isbister

Introduction

For the past 36 years, I have been involved in Aboriginal education. As a teacher, principal and director, I have been perplexed about the relationship between Aboriginal people and the European educational system. To say the least, there are bicultural and bilingual implications in this exchange. My suspicions bore fruit, however, when I became a participant in the post-gradate degree program. Studies emanating from the social science discipline revealed much more than I had anticipated. Some studies revealed that Aboriginal people were included in the plan to achieve a homogeneous society in Canada. What is alarming is that some studies revealed a difference in the application of pedagogical practices between traditional and contemporary Aboriginal people. It is this difference that caught my attention. What precipitated this change? Obviously, Aboriginal people have changed! This paper, then, will address this change, elucidate the results of this discrepancy and advocate the inclusion of Aboriginal pedagogy into the structures of public education.

Source

The information about traditional Aboriginal pedagogical practices has been secured from the oral tradition of elders and from two experiences I have had with elders.

During my 36 years as an educator for various educational authorities, I have had the pleasure and privilege of meeting elders from various reservations across Saskatchewan. In these encounters, elders have impressed and planted the Aboriginal "spirit" in me. Their counsel and wisdom will remain in the recesses of my subconscience. When issues about Aboriginal people are discussed, flashes of their teachings come to the surface. They appear as clear as day. The circumstance may be vivid, but identification cannot be ascertained. I approached a teacher-colleague of mine, a friend and an elder, about this handicap. Smith Atimayoo counselled, "We may not be able to identify the person who said this or that. In an oral society, the Cree culture places emphasis on what is said and less upon who said it." In keeping with the oral Cree tradition, then, less emphasis will be placed upon identification and more on the "content" of what is said. It is, therefore, from this perspective that traditional Aboriginal pedagogical practices will be presented.

At this juncture, I have a fear about what I am about to do—a fear that I might misquote, misinterpret or give an improper translation. If credence is placed on the "content," then I am confident that the elders will be satisfied with the message they have left with me and which I am going to share with you. The message was acquired in 1989 when I was a university student. At the time, the Saskatchewan Indian Cultural College sponsored a series of lectures on Cree culture. For a six-week period, there were two lectures a week delivered by elders from various reservations across Saskatchewan.

During one of these lectures I had an embarrassing, but illuminating, experience with Jim Kanapotatao, Elder from Onion Lake. Ignorant, but eager to learn about my Cree culture and heritage, I equipped myself with a tape recorder and a note pad. As I entered the room, Jim motioned me to sit beside him. He studied me as I prepared my equipment. When I completed the arrangement, he spoke in Cree:

> Grandchild, you should have more confidence in the faculties and senses bestowed upon you by the Creator. The mind, eyes and ears, when used to capacity, facilitate the learning process. Machine learning, on the other hand, dulls our capacity to learn and takes away the essence of the moment. This very moment is crucial; therein lies the truth. Truth is yesterday's problem and tomorrow's lies. Learn, then, my grandchild by use of your faculties and senses and you will discover the beauty and essence of the moment.

In humiliation, I took the equipment out of the room, but remained resolved to facilitate the learning process. I learned the significance and validity of oral tradition and that true learning occurs if we have the capacity to use our faculties and senses.

Another encounter I experienced was with my great-grandfather. At sunrise, this old man would walk around, touching this and that, looking into the four distant horizons, up to the sky and finally at the ground. This ceremony would last approximately 30 minutes. Again, at sundown, this old man would repeat the same ceremony, come rain or shine, snow or sleet. Intrigued by his actions, I asked for an explanation:

> Grandchild, I am praying to the Creator. I am thankful to be alive
> to witness the magnificence and benevolence of Mother Earth. All
> these things provided by the Creator. But, I am human, and,
> therefore, I am weak. Sometimes I forget why I am alive and why I
> am on Mother Earth. I, therefore, pray to the Creator for strength
> and wisdom. Strength to do His Will and wisdom to learn from
> nature what the Creator wants me to do.

Traditionally, then, Aboriginal people were mindful of the obligation to pay homage to the Creator on a daily basis. Prayer becomes an individual ceremony. It reveals the extent to which Aboriginal people revered the Creator and creation.

ABORIGINAL PARADIGMS

The following world-views or paradigms, which originated from the six-week workshop on Cree culture, are common to many Aboriginal cultures:

1. The universe, creation and all entities, including life itself, are gifts from the Creator (Elders, 1989).
2. a) Man, of all the entities in Creation, was last to be created. Man, then, learns from older, wiser entities (Deloria, 1991).
   b) To distinguish man from other entities, the Creator bestowed upon man the faculty "to think." If the mind is left to its own devices, it can become destructive. Learning from older, wiser entities entails observance of the "natural laws" of nature (Elders, 1989).
3. a) The natural laws of nature are those observable, natural phenomenon. They are perfect, prevalent and predicable since they are the Creator's Spirit in nature. These are balance, purpose, peace and harmony (Elders, 1989).

b) Four faculties constitute man: spirit, thought, feelings and actions
(Hampton, 1995). The "spirit" of man is paramount, since it emulates
the Creator's purpose; the other faculties of thought, feelings and
action are secondary, but are also important since they also express the
understanding of the Creator's purpose. As expressions of
understanding, each faculty is expected to emulate balance, purpose,
peace and harmony (Elders, 1989).

4. Each man, woman and child is expected to find the Creator's purpose.
It lies hidden in nature. The Creator reveals this secret incrementally.
Therefore, each man, woman and child must be diligent and observant.
(Highwater, 1981; Sioui, 1992).

Upon these world-views or paradigms, traditional Aboriginal pedagogical
practices are based.

COLONIAL PLAN TO ACHIEVE A CANADIAN HOMOGENEOUS SOCIETY

The traditional Aboriginal pedagogical practices came to an abrupt halt
when the European arrived on the North American continent. During
colonial times, the Canadian architects of nationhood devised a plan to
create a homogeneous society. To achieve cultural hegemony meant that all
ethnic groups, regardless of race, status or religious affiliation were to
receive the same education. It was anticipated that equality of education
would circumvent cultural barriers. Obviously, Aboriginal people were
included in this plan, but an assessment of the inclusion plan was plagued
with doubt. The architects of nationhood felt that Aboriginal people could
not be trusted if left to their own devices. Neither could Aboriginal people
educate themselves to become equal partners in the quest for nationhood.
Consequently, the state solicited the services of the Church. Hence, a
double-barrelled approach to the Aboriginal issue was taken.

APPLICATION OF PLAN FOR ABORIGINAL PEOPLE

The state, armed with a sequential curriculum premised on maximizing
European ideology, attempted to "Canadianize" Aboriginal people. The
Church, armed with Christian theology, promulgated a doctrine to baptize
Aboriginal people on the premise that the salvation of their souls would
"Christianize" Aboriginal people. Obviously, the double-barrelled

approach to Canadianize and to Christianize meant the complete negation of Aboriginal tradition and culture.

A Typical Initial Reaction in an Aboriginal/European Classroom

It is difficult to present the atmosphere of classrooms across Canada in which there are bilingual and bicultural implications. Under normal conditions, the teacher is compelled to follow a curriculum steeped in European ideology. Under compulsory education, the student is armed with Aboriginal tradition and culture. To illustrate a typical reaction of what did happen, both Highwater (1981) and Sioui (1992) share a similar experience:

> "Your ancestors," said the imposing Mother Superior who taught us history, "were savages with no knowledge of God. They were ignorant and cared nothing about their salvation." And, then, with a sincerity that sometimes had her close to tears, "The King of France took pity on them and sent missionaries who tried to convert them, but your ancestors, the savages, killed those missionaries, who became the blessed Canadian martyrs. Now, thanks to God and His Church, you are civilized people. You must ask God's pardon every day for the sins of your ancestors, and thank Him for introducing you to the Catholic faith, for snatching you from the hands of the Devil who kept your ancestors in a life of idolatry, theft, lying, and cannibalism. Now get down on your knees, we're going to pray to the blessed Canadian martyrs." [Sioui, 1992, introduction]

It appears that this typical reaction dichotomized the classroom atmosphere and environment. The children are presumably there "to learn" and the Mother Superior is there "to convert." In this way, the dichotomy is generalized. Mother Superior holds the premise that it is necessary "to save souls" so that the learning/teaching process can be facilitated when Aboriginal children are involved.

Results of Imposition

Compulsory education and a curriculum that emphasized European ideology was imposed upon Aboriginal people. What affect did this sustained process of imposition have upon Aboriginal people? Social science studies indicate that each generation of Aboriginal children began to look upon their culture as inferior and to look upon cultures outside the reservation as superior. These are indications that Aboriginal children are negating their cultures and donning the mantle of "Europeanism." There is also a tendency for the Canadian public, as well as the "assimilated" Aboriginal community, to shun Aboriginals who claim and profess to be Aboriginal. Personally, I have witnessed Aboriginal people oscillating between cultures to suit the demands of circumstance or to appease modern times. Collectively considered, then, this no-win situation renders Aboriginal people as unstable, suffering from a condition that Cajete (1994) describes as "cultural schizophrenia."

The architects of public education implemented their equal opportunity to education philosophy across schools in Canada. Many minority language groups, including Aboriginal people, participated. When the dust cleared and the results were tabulated, the architects found that the success rate of Aboriginals to be the lowest when results were compared with other minority language groups across Canada (Cummins, 1981). When it came to analyzing the cause of this dismal statistic, the architects concluded that there was nothing wrong with the system. Consequently, "blaming the victim" became the justification for the status quo in the education of Aboriginal people.

This "blaming the victim" concept, continued by the architects of public education, conveys two implications to the general public: first, that large sums of public funds are to be poured into Aboriginal education, and secondly, that "x" number of teachers have been hired for Aboriginal education. On the flip side, Aboriginal people are labelled as: a) ignorant because a majority of the children are obtaining a failing grade; b) lacking appreciation because Aboriginal people are not thankful for the "free" education, nor do they appreciate the time and effort of teachers; and c) unresponsive because they respond passively to government initiatives. This dichotomy is a condition that Hampton (1995) calls "a pathological complex," which describes the struggles of unconscious process that Aboriginal children encounter in the structures of public education:

(1) a perverse ignorance of the facts of racism and oppression;
(2) delusions of superiority motivated by a fear of inadequacy;

(3) a vicious spiral of self-justifying actions, as the blame is shifted to the victim who must be helped, that is, controlled for their own good;

(4) denial that the oppressor profits from the oppression materially, as well as casting themselves as superior, powerful and altruistic persons. [Hampton, 1995, p. 32]

EVALUATION

Two valid conclusions can be drawn:

1. The structures of public education premised on maximizing European ideology will continue to function and operate in Canadian schools, despite the negative impact upon Aboriginal children;

2. The negative impact of the structures of public education upon Aboriginal children has resulted in an unconscious negation of their "aboriginality." Aboriginal children have learned to feel like a European, act like a European, think like a European and believe in Christianity.

CONCLUSION

Time and time again, there have been studies, royal commissions and social experiments conducted upon Aboriginal people. European concerns, based upon European ideology, developed the parameters for a European resolution in anticipation of meeting European expectations. These endeavours have precipitated a dichotomy between indignant European philanthropists and Aboriginal people labelled as ignorant, unappreciative and unresponsive. Rather than merge their cultures, these well-laid plans have polarized these cultures, with each jealously protecting its domain.

Would it not be desirable to embrace compatible cultures, each promoting compassion for human diversity, rather than perpetuate conformity which prolongs confrontation and polarization? If we accept this, then change to the status quo is imminent. In anticipation of change, therefore, I present a personal experience. I have been counselled by educators and missionaries during my formative years that "happiness" can be secured by acquiring an education that makes it easier to acquire material necessities. I have acquired both an education and material necessities. I waited for that utopian state of happiness to come knocking on my door. Instead, misery became my constant companion. In the search of happiness, therefore, I resorted to the use of alcohol to be rid of my constant companion. Finally, misery and alcoholism paved the road toward apathy. On the periphery of apathy, I tried many European remedies, including the A.A. program, and detoxification and rehabilitation centres. These remedies did not resolve my predicament. Please do not misunderstand me: these remedies are beneficial—they do help "alcoholics" recover from their ailment. However, in my case, the process of conformity did not appeal to me. I did not want to participate in this society as another assimilated Aboriginal functioning from a preconceived and prescribed "pigeon hole" (Cecil, 1989). I wanted to be me.

To be me required the examination of who I was. In the quiet of my solitude, I began to assess my faculties. I was able to ascertain the following:

I had been thinking like a European.

I had been feeling like a European.

I had been acting like a good little European.

Over these years, I had been European. Almost immediately, I began to embrace my thoughts, my feelings and my actions. I have—finally—found happiness.

It is from this perspective I offer the proposal to include Aboriginal pedagogy in the structures of public education as a foundation.

It is obvious that a massive change is necessary to accommodate this. Two major changes are required. The first is that the Aboriginal concept of "spirit" must be accommodated. Second, the educational system must become more responsive to the unique way Aboriginal children perceive the world. The educational system has taught Aboriginal children to think like Europeans, to feel like Europeans and to act like Europeans. As products of the system, Aboriginal adults have learned to think, feel and behave as if their Aboriginality is inferior. A truly inclusive educational system will teach each Aboriginal child to develop an appreciation and responsiblity for his or her faculties of thought.

ACKNOWLEDGEMENTS

I would like to thank all those elders who participated in the six-week workshop on Cree culture in February, 1989.

REFERENCES

Cajete, G. (1994). *Look to the Mountain: An Ecology of Indigenous Education.* Durango, Colorado: Kivaki Press.

Cummins, J. (1981). *Bilingualism and Minority-Language Children.* Toronto: O.I.S.E. Press.

Deloria, V., Jr. (1991). *Traditional Technology: Indian Education in America.* Boulder, Colorado: American Indian Science and Engineering Society.

Elders (1989).
- Smith Atimoyoo, Little Pine Reserve, Director of the Saskatchewan Indian Cultural College
- Jim Kanapatatoe, Onion Lake Reserve — "Aboriginal Creation Belief"; "The Faculties of Man and the Natural Laws of Nature"
- John B. Tootoosis, Poundmaker Reserve — "Mother Earth" from the Aboriginal and the European perspectives; "Aboriginal Councept of Ownership"
- John Skeboss, Poorman Reserve — "Since the Creator Makes the Universe He Left His Spirit in Nature"
- Joe Duquette, Mistawasis Reserve — "The Concept of Respect"
- Edward Fox, Sweetgrass Reserve — "Each People Has a Purpose and Why This Must be Honoured"

Hampton, Eber. (1995). "Towards a Re-definition of American Indian Education." In Marie Battiste and Jean Barman, eds., *First Nations Education in Canada: The Circle Unfolds*, pp. 5–46. Vancouver: UBC Press.

Highwater, J. (1981). *The Primal Mind: Vision and Reality in Indian America.* New York: Penguin Book.

King, Cecil. (1989). "Here Comes the Anthros." Paper presented at the 88th Annual Meeting of the American Anthropological Association, Washington, D.C. November 18, 1989.

Sioui, G. E. (1992). *For an AmerIndian Auto History.* Kingston, Ontario: McGill-Queen's University Press.

An Analysis of Western, Feminist and Aboriginal Science Using the Medicine Wheel of the Plains Indians*

Lillian E. Dyck

This paper was originally titled "Putting the Woman and the Aboriginal into the Scientist: A Female Urban Indian Scientist's Perspective." This is rather masculinist language; now, I think the more appropriate title is "Honouring the Aboriginal Woman in the Scientist."

While preparing this paper for the Women and Other Faces in Science Conference, Saskatoon, Saskatchewan, September 1996, I had difficulties organizing and focusing my thoughts and realized that this was because I was not sure which style of language to use: the language of the scientist, the feminist or the Aboriginal. I speak all three languages.[1] Neuroscience is my area of science: I have researched how the brain uses chemical transmitters and how drugs, particularly antidepressants, affect neurotransmission; I have also investigated alcohol metabolism and most recently the biodistribution and metabolism of new aliphatic propargylamine drugs that hold promise of being neuronal rescue drugs. I am a feminist, knowledgeable about feminist and other critiques of Western or Eurocentric science.[2] I was raised in mainstream Canadian prairie culture and have recently begun to incorporate Aboriginal ideology into my thinking and practice. As chair of "Women and Other Faces in Science," I built in a session devoted to Aboriginal voices that provided an atmosphere of safety where I began to speak from an integrated place—as an Aboriginal woman—not just as a scientist who normally speaks as an objective authority and removes herself from the spoken or written word.

Mainstream North American culture maintains stereotypical images about what a scientist looks like and how a scientist conducts research.

---

*Reprinted, with permission, from *Native Studies Review* 11, no. 2 (1996)

What springs to mind are images of a man in a white lab coat pursuing research rationally and objectively and whose findings lead to an elucidation of universal truths. The public usually assumes that scientific enquiry is not affected by the scientist's preconceptions (scientists are considered selfless and objective) and the scientific method itself is thought to be immune from bias, so scientific experiments are thought to lead inevitably to indisputable results.

As a result, the identity of the scientist is considered unimportant. Thus, the underrepresentation of women or racial minorities is not seen to be a problem in terms of the kinds of research conducted. To illustrate how holding feminist or Aboriginal world-views can, in fact, affect scientific practice, this paper will briefly describe the traditional Western scientific method, examine assumptions inherent in it and highlight the influence of the investigator or scientist on research. Then it will describe how feminist and Aboriginal beliefs change the traditional view. Finally, science will be examined using the medicine wheel of the Plains Indians.

The traditional or textbook concept of Western science[3] is as follows:

- The scientist is completely separate from her object of investigation (e.g., rats, subatomic particles).
- The scientific method is infallible, exact and accurate.
- The scientist is unbiased, objective and impartial.
- Scientific knowledge is value-free.

Is this concept an illusion? A delusion? The truth?

The Oxford English Dictionary defines science and scientists as follows: Science is the "physical or natural sciences, collectively"; a natural science is "one dealing with material phenomena and based mainly on observation, experiment and induction—as chemistry, biology, physical science." A scientist is a "person with expert knowledge of a (usually physical or natural) science" or a "person using scientific methods." The definition of a scientist is embedded in the definition of natural science. This creates the illusion that natural science exists independently from the scientist. The scientist who makes the material phenomena known to herself and to us by observation and experimentation is not acknowledged. Similarly, we scientists use communication styles that create an illusion that we are separate from our science. We render ourselves invisible by eliminating the first person: instead of "I observed that the rats treated with drug 'x' were startled more easily than those treated with drug 'y'. . . ," we say "Drug 'x' resulted in. . . ."

Some definitions of the scientific method do not even mention the scientist as the agent carrying out the various steps in the scientific method:

1. the formulation of a hypothesis.
2. the design of an experiment to test the hypothesis—method to observe, measure, identifying variables, random sampling.
3. execution of the experiment.
4. analysis of the data.
5. judgement of the hypothesis.
6. generalization—conclusion, involving inductive reasoning.[4]

Clearly, a person is involved in every step, so an alternative view of Western science exposes the scientist and points out that the scientific method is subject to the scientist's biases; the scientist is imbedded in the research; the scientist has whatever biases pervade her culture. Scientific knowledge, by this view, is not value-free but a product limited by and tainted with the values of the culture that produces it.

Thus, scientists help present science as static through our acceptance of the belief in the infallibility of the scientific method and through our style of communication. Kuhn would describe this behaviour as part of our informal training as scientists: we and we alone learn the unwritten rules of our enterprise.

This simple introduction has focused on the roles of individual scientists, but Kuhn examines in depth the practice of science by the scientific community as a whole. He points out with clarity and eloquence how the ever-changing face of science, our constantly evolving knowledge of nature, is hidden or made invisible in the way textbooks are written and the way in which scientists are trained.[5] Science textbooks, which he claims are the main pedagogic instrument for training in science, are written from the perspective of the currently accepted theories; in rewriting or revising, the perspective of the old knowledge is removed as though it did not exist. For example, before Copernicus, the earth's moon was regarded as a planet and any observations of it were interpreted from that perspective; after

Copernicus was accepted, the moon was regarded as a satellite orbiting Earth, and all subsequent observations were interpreted and all previous observations reinterpreted from the new perspective.[6] In this way, the perspective of science is presented to the public as having always been as it is; as a *fait accompli*; as static, unchanging, immune to error.

According to Kuhn, studies of the history of science show that the scientific method is not sufficient to produce "unique, substantive conclusion." In fact, a number of incompatible conclusions may be reached by using the same method but asking different questions.[7] Furthermore, he notes that sufficient accumulation of these inconsistencies eventually leads to the overthrow of accepted scientific theory, usually via another type of science, which he calls revolutionary or creative science.[8] Scientists whose perspective is grounded in the old paradigm or theory think one way; those whose data are inconsistent with the old paradigm think differently because they view the problem while being immersed in the process of generating a new paradigm. In other words, revolutionary science occurs when anomalous findings (findings that are not consistent with accepted theory) are discovered and consensus (about rejecting the current theory) within the scientific community has not been reached. Kuhn states that, when the old beliefs are rejected, a new set of problems and standards to judge validity are adopted by the science community as a whole.[9] Normal science, then, resumes once again, until new anomalies are discovered. The process of science, then, is a continual cycle of normal science interspersed with revolutionary science.

Perhaps the greatest blow to the textbook view of Western science in modern times has come from physics, a science thought to be the gold standard of linear, reductionist science. The discovery that subatomic particles behave unpredictably, or with uncertainty, and that they appear to influence one another's behaviour (i.e., they behave neither predictably nor independently as single units whose properties can be studied and characterized in isolation from each other) make it evident that traditional concepts of science need to be modified to include such observations.

Feminist scholars have also challenged traditional concepts of Western science.[10] Feminist scientists "acknowledge that they, like everyone else, have values and beliefs and that these affect how they practice their science."[11] Feminist scientists openly acknowledge that they have biases affecting the research questions they propose, interpretation of their results and the conclusions they reach. Feminist science is seen in the context of the society—the social or cultural environment—in which it is carried out. They make their values and beliefs known; they do not adopt a stance of neutrality. Moreover, they have as a goal the use of their research to obtain women's equality. Women in the (social) community are seen to be an integral part of the research team, as collaborators in proposing projects and carrying out research. Feminist scientists are accountable to the community. Feminist science is non-hierarchic—a science "with the people, by the people and for the people," according to Margaret Benston.[12] The goal is to create knowledge grounded in women's experiences—virtually all Western science has been grounded in men's experiences.[13]

The question, "What is Aboriginal science?" is more difficult; little is written on the topic.[14] One way to answer it would be to talk about what was known by our ancestors in fields such as astronomy, agriculture and medicine. However, my intent here is to focus on the process of Aboriginal science. What were the traditional (ancestral) ways of knowing? Having been raised in white society, I am not schooled in traditional Aboriginal ways. Furthermore, some aspects of Aboriginal knowledge are sacred and learned by an extensive process of training with an elder; this knowledge is not shared with others publicly unless elders from that community decide it is right to do so. What I will do in this paper is to examine the way I, as a Western-trained scientist, do science using the medicine wheel of the Plains Indians as a framework for analysis.

The concepts embraced by the medicine wheel are an integral part of Plains cultures. It can be used to understand ideas, to show how all things are living and interconnected.[15] Everything is considered to have four aspects: spiritual, emotional, physical and mental. For example, a person in considered to be in balance or in harmony when each of these four aspects is equally developed. A person is whole when the opposite yet related aspects of the wheel are in balance (physical in balance with spiritual, mental in balance with emotional).

Tables 1 through 3 summarize the learning processes, the thinking processes and vision of Western science, feminist science and Aboriginal science as I see them with respect to their location in the medicine wheel. Differences among these three can be seen by comparing the characteristics listed.

Traditional Western science displays many attributes that can be designated as the mental, physical and emotional aspects of the medicine wheel (Figure 1), and many scientists like myself were attracted to research careers because of an intense curiosity (emotional and intellectual aspects) to understand how the material world operates from a reductionist perspective (physical aspect) and an ability to master the methods (tools, equipment) (physical aspect) used in research. We isolate and take things apart and selectively manipulate single variables to figure out how something works (physical aspect). The intellectual or mental aspects of science in terms of linear, reductionist thinking is well developed, but in terms of integrated logical and intuitive thinking or in terms of postulating interconnected models rather than linear models, it is not well developed. In traditional Western science, there is no spiritual domain.

Feminist science (as well as ecological and environmental sciences), in contrast to traditional Western science, is more conscious of the complexity of the material world. It could be said that feminist science and these other scientific disciplines are more balanced in that their intellectual aspect has been developed to include non-linearity,[16] plus a patent awareness of the biases and influence of the scientist on the research itself (see Table 2).

Aboriginal science (see Table 3) openly advocates a spiritual aspect; none of the alternative ways of doing science (feminist, ecological or environmental sciences) do so.

How does one cultivate the creative or spiritual aspects of doing science? This is the interesting question that I leave with you. All I can offer now as an answer is that it requires a scientist who incorporates spiritual practices into her/his personal life and thus has the tools to apply to her/his professional scientific life.

The creative aspect of Western science is largely undefined and invisible. Western science is thought to have no creative domain.

Table 1: Analysis of Western Science

East (physical aspect)

Learning A process of acquiring scientific knowledge in terms of:
   the language—written or published material
   the methods—what they are and the physical carrying out of experiments
   use of the physical senses, tools, pieces of equipment to observe and conduct supervised experiments; hands-on science.

Vision Focused like the mouse—vision is limited to what is nearby, but able to see clearly separate objects in a complex environment.

Thinking Atomistic, reductionistic, linear, step by step.

South (emotional aspect)

Learning By experimentation—the active stage of producing scientific knowledge.
   Able to design own experiments, speculate, solve problems, analyze.
   Passionate involvement in the practice of science.
   Science is fun.
   Enmeshment with research possible, biases unacknowledged.

Vision Ability to see a bigger picture than from the perspective of the East; still coloured with personal perspective.

Thinking Authoritarian, linear, logical, black and white.
   Opposites are in conflict with each other.
   I'm right, you're wrong (judgemental).
   Dualistic thinking—all-or-none thinking.

West (spiritual-creative aspect)

Non-existent.

North (mental/intellectual aspect)

Learning At the wisdom stage—acquired with experience.
   Learning integrates knowledge from the physical and emotional aspects but not the other two aspects of the wheel.
   The scientist works alone or as a separate individual in group work.

Vision Limited, not detached from personal investments.

Thinking No integration of reason and intuition.
   Authoritarian, judgemental.
   Ethical and moral aspects of scientific practices considered to be of little or no relevance.

However, Kuhn considers revolutionary or creative science to be essential to the growth or development of new scientific theories; leaps forward do not occur by the linear, reductionist methods of Western science.[17] In my opinion, it is the methods of creative science that have been made invisible to the scientific and non-scientific communities. I was happy to see that Kuhn mentioned, albeit briefly, that intuition and illumination during sleep were the methods of problem-solving employed in creative science.[18] What was of paramount significance for me on reading his essay was the recognition that the big leaps in scientific thinking occurred via revolutionary science—through dreams, intuition, sudden insight from out of the blue.

Table 2: Analysis of Feminist and Other Alternative Sciences

East
Same as Western science.

South
Same as Western science.

West
Non-existent, same as Western science.

North (mental/intellectual aspect)
Learning is at the wisdom stage—acquired with experience.

> Learning by integration of knowledge acquired from the emotional, physical and intellectual aspects of the wheel.
> Balanced learning—seeing that things are connected non-linearly.[19]
> The scientist works synergistically in group or collaborative work, with diverse perspectives on a problem and diverse ways of thinking leading to new insights.
> Awareness of the need for community input and the impact of science on the community (persons and environment).[20]

Vision   Broad perspective, detached from personal opinion, set in the social context.

Thinking Combining diverse elements or perception (accepting, non-judgemental).
> Can see that all things fit together, are interconnected.[21]
> Ethical and moral aspects of scientific practices considered to be crucial.

Two examples of these creative methods, which were mere asides during my undergraduate chemistry lectures, have stuck in my brain to this day. Kekulé dreamt of a snake swallowing its tail when he was trying to figure out the chemical structure of benzene—the dream gave

---

Table 3: Analysis of Aboriginal Science

East
Same as Western and feminist science.

South
Same as Western and feminist science.

West (spiritual-creative aspect)

Learning	By use of intuition—an openly advocated, accepted way of knowing.
	Going within stage, a time of inner contemplation (hibernation of the bear).
	Accessing information from the subconscious realm of our beings.
	Active listening to our gut hunches, intuition, dreams and spirit helpers to provide insights into problem-solving in the physical realm.
Vision	Far-seeing as the eagle; intuitive insight developed.
Thinking	Creative, open to intuitive insights.
	Flexible—non-perfectionist, balance rather than dualism.
	Opposites define or compliment each other.
	Ability to see patterns of relationships that are non-linear.

North
Same as for Western and feminist science, plus:

Learning	At the wisdom stage—acquired with experience.
	Learning by integration of knowledge acquired from all aspects of the wheel, including the spiritual aspect.
	Balanced learning—seeing that all things are connected[22]
	to imagine, to interpret
	to see the connections
	to use intuition (hunches, insight) consciously.
Vision	Broad perspective, detached from personal opinion and informed by spiritual insight.
Thinking	Active integration of intuition and reason.

him the insight to look at a ring structure. Similarly, Mendeleyev used playing cards to sort out the relationship between the chemical properties of elements and their atomic weights, and came up with the periodic table.

The individual scientist plays a role in hiding the existence of these other "scientific" methods. For instance, the solution to a problem might come in the form of a night-time dream to a scientist, but that insight alone is not acceptable scientific proof or evidence. What happens is that the insight from the dream gives the scientist the perspective from which to design an appropriate experiment to provide scientifically acceptable evidence. When the research is completed and

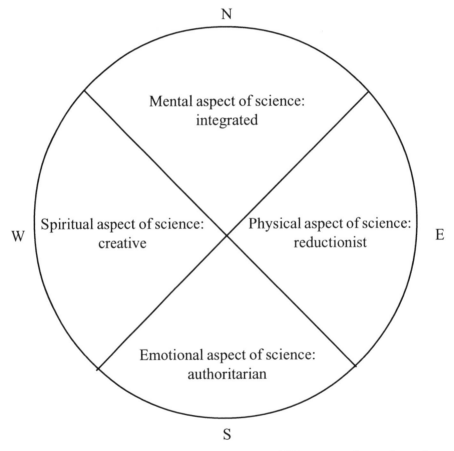

Figure 1: Placing the thinking processes of Western science into the medicine wheel

written up for publication, the insight of the dream is not described in the methods or the discussion. There may be reluctance in revealing publicly the "unscientific" process of creative insight. What is clear to me as a scientist, though, is that this type of science—the big leaps forward in thinking—is what is most exciting and what many of us strive to attain.

If we call these unusual methods of problem solving *creative*, they likely will be acceptable to every scientist; however, the adjective *spiritual* would be rejected. For centuries, philosophers have debated the existence of a spiritual world; in Aboriginal culture, there is no debate. The spiritual and physical worlds both exist, and it is from the former that our creative insights and dream messages originate.

This analysis of Western, feminist and Aboriginal science using the medicine wheel comes from my limited understanding as an urban Indian raised outside of my Plains Cree culture. I am relatively young with respect to my journey of learning about my Cree heritage from various Teachers, so when it was pointed out to me that I had erred in placing the spiritual aspect of the medicine wheel in the west rather than the east, I was not surprised. The east is the place of entry into the medicine wheel—it is the spiritual beginning. We are born into this world as pure spirits. My upbringing in Eurocentric society and training in Western science have conditioned me to think of the physical domain as the logical starting place, so I placed the physical aspect of science in the east. I was aware of this anomaly, since the diagram in the Sacred Tree shows the spiritual aspect in the east of the wheel, but my mind was not able to accept this placement—yet.

Perhaps in time, as I begin to understand the spiritual aspect of science and its practitioners better, I will be able to place it in the east. Undoubtedly, those people who choose to go into science because they wish to understand the mysteries and complexities of the universe would have no difficulty placing the spiritual aspect of science in the east position (Figure 2). Those who were attracted to science by a deep love of nature and the desire to do something soulful rather than mundane—who study astronomy or biology to gain a glimpse of the interconnectedness and mysteries of life—clearly have spiritual and not simply intellectual reasons for their scientific enquiries. When I was in

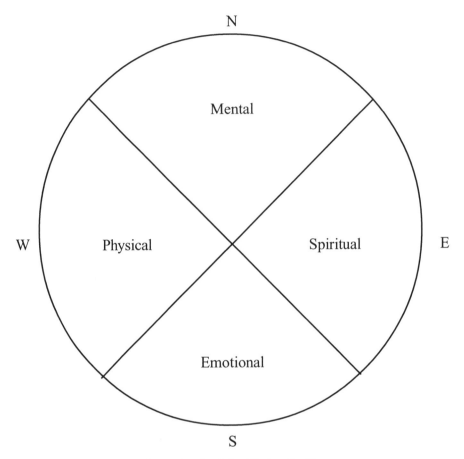

Figure 2: The medicine wheel of the Plains Indians

grade school, that was what intrigued me about science; however, as I grew older and adapted to the education system, I developed my intellectual abilities intensively, but that other part of me, the spiritual-creative part, was shut away and is only now slowly resurfacing.

ACKNOWLEDGEMENTS

This paper is dedicated to my mother, Eva Muriel McNab (1920–1956). She was a Cree Indian from the Gordon's Reserve near Punnichy, Saskatchewan. Provincial laws, federal laws and racism prevented her from living as a traditional Cree woman. She left the reserve and married Yok Leen Quan, my father. In her own time, in her own way, she was a feminist from whom I received courage and determination. In 1981, I obtained a Ph.D., and then, at age 36, I began the search for my Cree heritage. I thank my Teachers and Helpers on this path.

NOTES

1 The styles, vocabulary and meanings of certain words, written or spoken, may vary between specialized subgroups. Thomas Kuhn also used the metaphor of language to describe the communication gap between "men who hold incommensurable viewpoints" who are like "members of different language communities"; *The Structure of Scientific Revolutions*, 2nd ed. (Chicago, University of Chicago Press, 1970), p. 175.

2 Many articles, from Kuhn's classic treatise cited above to a range of feminist scholars (philosophers, historians of science and scientists) criticize science, especially its stance on being objective and value-free. It is not my intention to review these papers, but I found several to be especially helpful: Ruth Bleier, "Introduction," in *Feminist Approaches to Science*, edited by R. Bleier (New York: Pergamon Press, 1988), pp. 1–17; Ursula Franklin, "Letter to a Graduate Student," *Canadian Woman Studies* 13 (1993): 12–15; Sue V. Rosser, "The Relationship between Women's Studies and Women in Science," in *Feminist Approaches to Science*, edited by R. Bleier (New York: Pergamon Press, 1988), pp. 165–180; M.H. Whatley, "Taking Feminist Science to the Class Room: Where Do We Go from Here?" in *Feminist Approaches to Science*, edited by R. Bleier (New York: Pergamon Press, 1988), pp. 181–190; Linda Christiansen-Ruffman, "Community Base and Feminist Vision—The Essential Grounding of Science in Women's Community," *Canadian Woman Studies* 13 (1993): 16–20; Roberta Mura, "Searching for Subjectivity in the World of the Sciences: Feminist Viewpoints," Canadian Research Institute for the Advancement of Women Papers no. 25; Evelyn Fox Keller, "Introduction," *Secrets of Life, Secrets of Death* (New York: Routledge, Chapman and Hall, Inc., 1992).

3 Kuhn, *The Structure of Scientific Revolutions*, describes the process of scientific discovery over time as a process of normal science punctuated intermittently with revolutionary science. Normal science is undertaken using methods and knowledge that are accepted by all members of the particular science community. This normal science is equivalent to what others have termed Western or Eurocentric science, and I have adopted the latter terms in this paper.

4 J.M. Little, *An Introduction to the Experimental Method* (Minnesota: Burgess Publishing Co., 1961).

5 Kuhn, "The Invisibility of Revolutions," *The Structure of Scientific Revolutions*, pp. 136–143.

6 Kuhn, "Revolutions as Changes of World View," *The Structure of Scientific Revolutions*, pp. 111–135.

7 Kuhn, "Introduction: A Role for History," *The Structure of Scientific Revolutions*, p. 3.

8 Kuhn, "Revolutions as Changes of World View," *The Structure of Scientific Revolutions*, pp. 111–135.

9 Kuhn, "Introduction: A Role for History," *The Structure of Scientific Revolutions*, p. 6.

10 See note 2.

11 Ruth Bleier, "Introduction," in *Feminist Approaches to Science*, edited by R. Bleier (New York: Pergamon Press, 1988), p. 15.

12 Margaret Benston (1937–1991) was a chemist and a Women's Studies scholar at Simon Fraser University; her legacy to women, science and technology was the theme for volume 13, number 2 of *Canadian Woman Studies*. Ursula Franklin and Linda Christiansen-Ruffman quote her (see footnote 2).

13 See footnote 2. An excellent example of feminist science is that carried out at the Centre pour l'étude des interactions biologiques entre la santé et l'environnement, Montreal, Québec. Donna Mergler gave an overview of occupational health research at the Women and Other Faces in Science Conference. One example of the centre's research was an investigation into domestic cleaners being exposed to toxic chemicals: a problem set in the social context of occupational health concerns that involved the workers themselves and their unions throughout the research study.

14 I am not aware of any books or papers that take the approach I have—i.e., using the medicine wheel as an analytic tool to examine Western science. I am aware of two books that have sections describing Aboriginal science or comparing it to Western science. Gregory Cajete, an Aboriginal scholar, wrote "Seven Orientations of Environmental Knowledge," in *Look to the Mountain: An Ecology of Indigenous Education* (Kivaki Press, 1994), pp. 193–207. F. David Peat, a non-Aboriginal physicist, wrote "Indigenous Science," in *Lighting the Seventh Fire: The Spiritual Ways, Healing and Science of the Native American* (Birch Lane Press, 1994), pp. 239–274.

15 For a detailed description of the concepts embodied in the medicine wheel, refer to J. Bopp et al. (producers), *The Sacred Tree* (Lethbridge, Alberta: Four Worlds Development Press, 1984).

16 See footnote 19.

17 Kuhn, *The Nature and Necessity of Scientific Revolutions*, pp. 122–123.

18 Kuhn, *The Nature and Necessity of Scientific Revolutions*, pp. 122–123.

19 Lea Bill, an Aboriginal nurse and researcher, presented a paper at the Women and Other Faces in Science Conference describing the process of collecting data in the form of oral histories from elders in northern Alberta. In Western science, the observations of such a group would not be considered valid scientific data because they were not collected by those trained within the scientific enterprise. Such a dismissal fails to recognize the skills these elders have developed within their own communities to note accurately and intelligently changes in their environment—the water, earth, air, insects, plants and animals. The strength of their observations is that they are seen as connected. Moreover, their observations, collected over many years, reveal connections related to time. Their evidence is not so concrete or specific as changes in the pH of the water as measured by a piece of scientific equipment; their science is more expansive in character. Their scientific evidence is to document by observation changes in their environment that occur over time: changes in plant life, numbers and/or type of fish, physical changes in fish or animals, and so on. Western science, on the other hand, which limits itself to intensive or detailed observations of isolated or single units of a complex system, would not have the range of observations, the contextual link nor the historical perspective.

20 See footnote 13.

21 See footnote 16.

22 Kuhn, *The Nature and Necessity of Scientific Revolutions*, pp. 92–110.

Aboriginal Pedagogy: Storytelling

MaryAnne Lanigan

Introduction

It is nothing short of a miracle that the First Nations of Canada have survived. A little battered and bruised, Canada's first peoples have managed to preserve their cultures in the face of constant onslaught from the dominant society—an onslaught that is premised on the vanishing-race image that has been perpetuated throughout history. This image, which developed in colonial times, led to the attitude that "the only good Indian was a dead Indian."

Population devastation due to disease and warfare gave the impression that indeed First Nations peoples were vanishing from the face of the Earth. First Nations populations declined continuously during the first 400 years of contact, until they reached their nadir early in the 20th century. This reality, coupled with the conceptions of progress and evolution, helped to support the orthodox social scientific theories. One of the major assumptions of all orthodox theories is that there is a duality of modern and primitive characteristics in our society, and through education the primitive peoples can be modernized. Modernization, of course, meant the discarding of traditional beliefs and practices, while accepting the cultural norms of the dominant society. In short, assimilation of First Nations cultures was and is a goal of dominant society education systems. Whether through death or assimilation, the result is the same: cultural genocide for Canada's First Nations.

It is this image that has led to the denial of First Nations as active participants in history, both before and after contact. It is this image that has served to marginalize First Nations from the socio-economic arena in Canada, starting with the establishment of the reservation system—a place where First Nations were sent to die or become assimilated. This was followed by missionary and residential schooling, which seemed to speed up the process of assimilation. The final assault continued with integrated schools, where the only accepted knowledge was that of the upper middle class of the dominant society. In spite of these assaults, First Nations have survived. Geoffrey York, in his book *The Dispossessed*, speaks of the fifth generation prophecy made by First Nations Chiefs at the signing of the treaties on the Canadian prairies in the 1870s. First Nations, starving, demoralized, pressured by white settlement and disease, were looking to the future, the fifth generation, for the revitalization and strengthening of First Nations cultures (York, 1989, p. 262). We are the fifth generation! The rebuilding has started and will continue through First Nations education, which will include both Aboriginal epistemology and pedagogy. As Judge Murray Sinclair said, in his speech to the Annual General Assembly of the Native Council of Canada in 1984:

> Aboriginal people are not without hope, for we are strong peoples.
> We have overcome seemingly insurmountable obstacles in our
> long and painful histories, because our creator has given us the
> tools necessary for our survival. We must not be shy to use them.
> We must no longer feel the shame and fear that our grandmothers
> and grandfathers felt about what we are and where we have come
> from. We must look to ourselves for our own guarantees, for we
> are the only ones that we can trust to ensure that our needs are met.
> [quoted in York, 1989, p. 271]

Our greatest need at present is to provide a relevant education that reflects the aboriginal world view and pedagogy.

LITERATURE REVIEW

Literature relating to First Nations education is a continuum moving from assimilation toward liberation. The orthodox assumption that progress means modernization, which in turn means conforming to the beliefs and values of the dominant society in Canada, is alive and well. Authors writing from this theoretical perspective have assimilation as their goal and see education as the tool to bring about uniformity of values and beliefs, which in turn will make Canada a better place for one and all, with equality of people and opportunity in the forefront. After giving various religious denominations the responsibility of educating First Nations peoples in Canada, the Canadian government turned a blind eye to the First Nations peoples' socio-economic conditions. It wasn't until the 1950s, when Farley Mowat wrote the novel *People of the Deer*, that Canadians became aware of the deplorable social conditions suffered by First Nations peoples in Canada (Mowat, 1954). Due to public outcry, the Canadian government undertook a number of studies to examine the socio-economic conditions of First Nations in Canada (most notably, Lagasse, 1959; Hawthorn, 1966). Education and training were seen as the major solution for improving social conditions. Thus began an intensive attempt to assimilate First Nations through education. Integrated schools were seen as the answer. Much of the literature in the 1980s and 1990s about First Nations is aimed at achieving the assimilationist goal. John Lee (1986), Rose Marcuzzi (1986), Jerline Quintal-Finell (1990) and J. P. Frideres and W. J. Reeves (1993) reflect the assimilationist goal. They all agree that First Nations students are unsuccessful in the Canadian education system. While recognizing the failure of the education system to meet the needs of Aboriginal students, these writers do not question the validity of the system itself. Their solutions aim at adopting strategies for success in a system that, to date, has not provided meaningful education to First Nations students. This is because this system is focused on the development of the English language and the dominant culture as a premise for intellectual development.

Others, such as Hap Gilliland (1992), Claudine Goller (1984), Karen Swisher and Donna Deyhle (1989), Mary Ellen Campbell (1991) and Jim Cummins (1992) discuss learning styles and examine ways of incorporating material and teaching strategies that capitalize on the Aboriginal way of learning. This is a step in the right direction, but is still not enough to guarantee meaningful learning experiences for First Nations children. The authors have made progress in their attitude towards First Nations. They are willing to allow for learning differences, but they, too, do not question the system itself. They, too, are working towards assimilation through education.

Freedom has been maintained by retaining cultural integrity, which has led to marginalization within the dominant society. We have now come full circle in First Nations education, as we are now looking to education not as a means of assimilation, but as a means of liberation. Vine Deloria (1991), Shirley Sterling (1995), Sharilyn Calliou (1995), Walter Lightning (1995),

Willie Ermine (1995), Eber Hampton (1995), Marie Battiste (1992), James Youngblood Henderson (1993) and Gregory Cajete (1994) are First Nations authors who are examining the education system and recognizing its inability to provide meaningful education for First Nations students. Instead of trying to adjust the system, they are investigating Aboriginal epistemology and pedagogy. Seeing the importance of retaining and passing on Aboriginal knowledge, as well as providing First Nations with the dominant society's knowledge, these writers are proposing the use of traditional pedagogies to impart both systems of education. The result is meaningful education that preserves a First Nations world-view at a time when all knowledge will be needed to repair and save the Earth for future generations.

ABORIGINAL PEDAGOGY

First Nations education is premised on the personal growth of the human being. It recognizes that learning begins with birth and continues until death. The individual learns how to be a good human being and then develops skills that will enable her/him to be a contributing member of society (Deloria, 1991, p. 21). We are seeing a re-emergence of traditional educational practices within First Nations communities. Traditional education, according to Hampton, includes "oral histories, teaching stories, ceremonies, apprenticeships, learning games, formal instruction, tutoring and tag-along teaching" (Hampton, 1995, p. 4). We are also witnessing an attempt to develop First Nations models and structures within non-Native structures. The inclusion of the First Nations forms of education gives value to the diversity of Canadian society for "it takes many of us to see more than [one side]" (Hampton, 1995, p. 37). First Nations pedagogy will provide a new way for non-Natives to view the world. Storytelling, common to all cultures as a method of teaching, is a First Nations pedagogy that can be revived in First Nations communities as well as fitted into non-Native education structures.

STORYTELLING

"We are all related" (Cajete, 1994, p. 74). This is especially true when we examine storytelling as a teaching tool. The oldest of the arts in every culture, storytelling is the basis of all intergenerational communication.

Cajete writes:

> Story—in creative combination with encounters, experiences,
> image making, ritual, play, imagination, dream and modeling—
> forms the basic foundation of all human learning and teaching.
> [Cajete, 1994, p. 68]

It is through story that children learn about themselves and their relationship to others. Charles A. Smith, after examining stories from many cultures, summarized that eight basic themes emerge:

- becoming a goal seeker
- confronting challenges courageously
- growing close to others
- coming to terms with loss and grief
- offering kindness to others
- preserving an openness to the world
- becoming a social problem solver
- forming a positive self-image [Smith, 1989]

It is through cultural stories that children learn how they fit in their world. Basil Johnston stated in 1977, "it is in a story that their fundamental understandings, insights and attitudes towards life and human conduct in all its forms are inscribed" (quoted in Verral, 1988, p. 7). It is through story that meaningful educational experiences will emerge for First Nations children.

The Cree word for mind is *mom-tune-ay-chi-kun*, which means "the sacred place inside, where we can dream, imagine, create and talk to the grandmothers and grandfathers" (Verral, 1988, p. 7). *Mom-tune-ay-chi-kuna*, translated to English as wisdoms, means "the thoughts and images that come from this place . . . [which] can be given to others in stories, songs, dances, and art. . . . All these are gifts that come from that sacred place inside" (Maria Campbell, quoted in Verral, 1988, p. 3). It is these sacred stories of First Nations peoples that provide insight into relationships through the understanding and appreciation of life and culture. They foster creativity and imagination that lead to the comprehension of the moral order inspiring the search for truth and wisdom (Verral, 1988, p. 7). Stories [teach] people who they are so they can become all they were meant to be (Cajete, 1994, p. 121).

There are two types of First Nations stories: myths and narratives. Myths are the sacred truths of a group of people. Strict protocol must be followed when telling myths. Only a prescribed storyteller should tell the sacred myths. These myths are only to be told during the winter. It is important that the myths be told accurately, so a training or apprenticeship is required. Each myth has more than one meaning. It is for the listener to think about and interpret the message. Cajete writes:

> Every myth has its concentric rings of meaning and is told and retold in this way. The telling of a myth begins with a simple version for children, then moves to a slightly more complicated version for adolescents, to a deeper version for initiates and to a still deeper version for the fully mature. [Cajete, 1994, p. 121]

An attentive listener will be able to view a myth from many sides and learn different things each time the myth is told. In time, the listener develops the creativity and intuition to look at ordinary experiences in a variety of new ways. A construct for the understanding of myths is as shown in Figure 1.

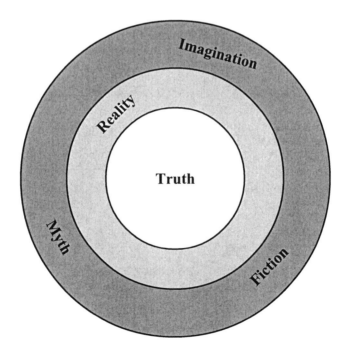

Figure 1. Construct for understanding myths

It is the cultural truths of First Nations Peoples that are found in myths. Lenore Keship-Tobias explains the telling of First Nations sacred stories:

Storytelling was never done for sheer entertainment, for the stories were and are a record of proud Nations confident in their achievements and their way of life. Stories contain information about tribal values, patterns of the environment and growing seasons, ceremonial or religious detail, social roles, geographical formations, factual and symbolic data, animal and human traits. [Tobias, quoted in Verral, 1988, p. 2]

The truths found in stories are essential to cultural continuity, so it is with seriousness that children are called to listen. Shirley Sterling describes the storytelling sessions with Yetko, her paternal grandmother:

After dark, she would gather all the kids around her call, 'choot-ka-hop'. The kids would say, 'hop'. That meant they were going to be quiet and listen to the story. If they didn't want to listen, they would have to go outside. They could play all they want and make noise out there. But nobody did. We all wanted to hear the stories she told. [Sterling, 1995, p. 114]

Stories that told of the world's beginning, its transformation to its present state, and the importance of maintaining a balance between animals and humans so that the world can be safe for all.

Time in myths can be represented by a circle divided into four parts, as shown in Figure 2.

The time has come for all humans to be reminded of the importance of taking care of the Earth and all creation for, indeed, "we are all related" (Cajete, 1994, p. 74).

In addition to myths, there are narratives that provide an oral account of the historical events of First Nations. These narratives were committed to memory. Edward Ahenekew attests to the accuracy of narratives told by the old men of the community:

An old man often had the gift of eloquence, enhanced by descriptive language and by superb mastery of gesture. He used his skill with natural simplicity, weaving into stories of everyday

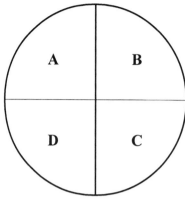

A. Animals and humans are enemies.
B. Transformation: Animals and humans achieve balance.
C. World is safe for humans.
D. Animals and humans share. Humans are reprimanded periodically for their self-centred arrogance that threatens all living beings.

Figure 2. Time in myths

events the primary meanings of life. The genius was most evident in the narration of past events, of raids and battles and the chase. He might bring a bit of comedy into a tragic story, touch it with pathos or sweeten it with love and loyalty—and do all this in a language highly figurative and yet suited to the subject; and his listeners would sit entranced, imagining that they saw and heard the events enacted before them—tales of struggles almost superhuman, of endurance, of perilous adventure, of long hazardous excursions into enemy country, of love, of anything indeed that was ever of any consequence in Indian life. All these stories were kept intact, unchanging, entrusted through the years by one generation to the next. [Ahenakew, 1973, p. 25]

Theirs was the ultimate responsibility, that of historian in oral society. It is only when these oral histories have been accepted can we begin to see the whole picture of the past.

Aside from historical narratives, there are also personal narratives—the narrative of families and their deeds. These narratives give pride and confidence to the young. Maria Campbell writes about the importance of this type of narrative in her story, "Dat Teef":

Hees not just dah stealing dats bad you know.
All dough dats bad enough.
Dah real bad ting is your kids and all your granchildren.
Dey don got no good stories about you if your a teef.

An dah stories you know
dats dah bes treasure of all to leave your family.
Everyting else on dis eart
he gets los or wore out.
But dah stories
dey las forever.
Too bad about dat man hees kids.
Jus too bad. [Campbell, 1995, pp. 143–145]

There are many First Nations who have done great deeds. These people are members of families. It is their stories that need to be told to children so that they can look to their past with pride and face the future with courage making new stories for the next generation.

STORYTELLING IN THE CLASSROOM

First Nation's stories, both myth and narrative, can be integrated across all subjects. To date, they are mostly used in language arts and social studies. Science is an area where the incorporation of First Nations stories could provide a wealth of information about plants and animals that are indigenous to Canada. Stories also bring the study of the solar system to a more personal level for students and can lead to greater understanding. Health, family life and religion are all areas where stories add greater depth and deeper understanding, for we learn how to be a good person and live a good life by listening attentively to First Nations sacred stories.

When using First Nations stories in the classroom, the teacher should know about the culture from which the stories originated. She/he should follow carefully the protocol associated with telling First Nations stories. There is a greater impact with students if they experience the stories orally. Stories are best told in a circle on the ground or floor remembering that the stories came from the Earth and contact with the Earth is important. A circle on the floor reminds the children that all creation is equal, for, in a circle, no one place is more important than another.

Another important aspect of storytelling is providing children with the context for comprehending the story. Knowing about characters, both animate and inanimate, and sharing this knowledge with the students before the formal storytelling session begins, captures their interest and motivates them to listen carefully. For example, when telling the story

"Wesakaychak and Wetiko" the storyteller should tell a little bit about each of the main characters, particularly about Wesakaychak. Weskaychak is the trickster character in Cree legends. This character embodies all that is characteristic of creation. It is "through trickster's transgressions as well as virtues that one learns, especially learning not to do as trickster has done" (Verral, 1988, p. 20). So it is important for the students to know ahead of time that Wesakaychak is curious, always hungry, loves to play tricks on the animals and has special powers. A short story about the origin of Wetiko should be told prior to the telling of the actual story. Ermine's characteristics are an integral part of the story, so it is only necessary to provide students with the common name for Ermine and a picture to help them visualize him in the story. In essence, a storytelling session involves telling several stories. This is the uniqueness of First Nations stories: they are all interconnected.

In an effort to show the importance of storytelling in the classroom, I choose two Cree stories, "Wesakaychak and Wetiko" (Appendix 1) and "Wesakaychak and the Killdeer" (Appendix 2). I told the first story orally within a story circle on the first day. The following day, I gave the students a question sheet about the story (Appendix 3). First thing on the third morning, I gave each student a copy of the second story to read. At the end of that day, the students were given a question sheet to complete (Appendix 3). The classes were a multicultural, multi-level group.

First, I found that all levels of students were equally successful at listening skills, comprehension skills and writing skills with the oral story. The students sat quietly, listened carefully, recalled information and were able to express their knowledge in written form. Second, the students appeared to have greater confidence in their ability after the oral stories. They approached the questions with enthusiasm and completed them in less time than the questions for the story they had read. Third, the students wrote more and expressed themselves more grammatically when answering the questions about the oral story. Fourth, all students performed better on the questions for the oral story than those for the story that was read silently. Fifth, students who were academically challenged showed the greatest discrepancy in successful answers for questions between the oral and written stories (see Appendix 4).

The results of this short study show the importance of storytelling for all students, but especially for students who are having difficulties academically. If we, as educators, want to motivate while building the self-esteem in our students, we need to develop skills in storytelling. Storytelling as a First Nations pedagogy is a necessary tool for achieving this goal.

SUMMARY

Storytelling is the oldest form of the arts. It is the basis of all other arts—drama, art, dance and music. It has been and is an important part of every culture. It is necessary for the revitalization of First Nations cultures and can be a starting point for moving away from assimilationist to liberationist education. Stories provide the intergenerational communication of essential ideas. Stories have many layers of meaning, giving the listener the responsibility to listen, reflect and then interpret the message. Stories incorporate several possible explanations for phenomena, allowing listeners to creatively expand their thinking processes so that each problem they encounter in life can be viewed from a variety of angles before a solution is reached. All people, young and old, love stories.

REFERENCES

Ahenekew, Edward. (1973). *Voices of the Plains Cree*. Toronto: McClelland and Stewart Ltd.

Battiste, Marie Ann. (1992). *Indigenous Epistemology in Modern Education and Thought*. University College of Cape Breton.

Berkhoffer, Robert F., Jr. (1978). *The Whiteman's Indian: Images of the American Indian from Columbus to the Present*. New York: Vintage Books.

Cajete, Gregory. (1994). *Look to the Mountain: An Ecology of Indigenous Education*. Durango, Colorado: Kivaki Press.

Calliou, Sharilyn. (1995). "Peacekeeping Actions at Home: A Medicine Wheel Model for a Peacekeeping Pedagogy." In Marie Battiste and Jean Barman, eds., *First Nations Education in Canada: The Circle Unfolds*, pp. 47–71 . Vancouver: UBC Press.

Campbell, Maria. (1995). *Stories of the Road Allowance People*. Penticton: Theytus Books Ltd.

Campbell, Mary Ellen. (1991). *The 5 B's of Success for Teaching Aboriginal Students*. Viewpoints monograph no. 5. Saskatoon: University of Saskatchewan, College of Education.

Cummins, Jim. (1992). "Empowering Indian Students: What Teachers and Parents Can Do." In Jon Reyhnes, ed., *Teaching American Indian Students*, pp. 301–317. Norman and London: University of Oklahoma Press.

Deloria, Vine, Jr. (1991). *Indian Education in America*. Boulder, Colorado: American Indian Science and Engineering Society.

Ermine, Willie. (1995). "Aboriginal Epistemology." In Marie Battiste and Jean Barman, eds., *First Nations Education in Canada: The Circle Unfolds*, pp. 101–112. Vancouver: UBC Press.

Frideres, J.P., and W.J. Reeves. (1993). "Indian Education: An Alternative Program." In Sonia Morris, Keith McLeod and Marcel Daneski, eds., *Aboriginal Languages and Education: The Canadian Experience*, pp. 37–53. Winnipeg: Mosaic Press.

Gilliland, Hap. (1992). "Growth Through Native American Learning Styles." *Teaching the Native American*. 2nd ed. Dubuque: Kendall/Hunt Publishing.

Goller, Claudine. (1984). "Teaching Native Students in an Urban Setting." *Multiculturalism* 7 (3): 17–20.

Hampton, Eber. (1995). "Towards a Re-definition of American Indian Education." In Marie Battiste and Jean Barman, eds., *First Nations Education in Canada: The Circle Unfolds*, pp. 5–46. Vancouver: UBC Press.

Hawthorn, H. B. (1966). *A Survey of the Contemporary Indians in Canada: A Report on Economic, Political, Educational Needs and Policies in Two Volumes*. Ottawa: Indian Affairs Branch.

Henderson, James Youngblood. (1993). *Governing the Implicate Order: Self-Government and the Linguistic Development of Aboriginal Communities*. Ottawa: University of Ottawa.

Lagasse, Jean H. (1959). *A Study of the People of Indian Ancestry in Manitoba*. 2 vols. Winnipeg: The Department of Agriculture and Immigration.

Lee, John. 1986. "Teaching Inner-City Adolescents" *Canadian Journal of Native Education* 13 (2): 22–26.

Lightning, Walter. (1995). "Compassionate Mind: Implication of a Text Written by Elder Louis Sunchild." In Marie Battiste and Jean Barman, eds., *First Nations Education in Canada: The Circle Unfolds*. Vancouver: UBC Press.

Marcuzzi, Rose. (1986). "Urban Education of Urban Indian Children" *Canadian Journal of Native Education* 13 (2): 27–31.

Mowat, Farley. (1954). *People of the Deer*. Toronto: MacMillan.

Quintal-Finell, Jerline. (1990). *Northern Saskatchewan Native Students' Readings and Storytellings of Culturally Relevant and Culturally Non-Relevant Stories*. Unpublished master's thesis, University of Saskatchewan, Saskatoon, Saskatchewan.

Smith, Charles A. (1989). *From Wonder to Wisdom: Using Stories to Help Children Grow*. New York: Nal Books.

Sterling, Shirley. (1995). "Quaslametko and Yetko: Two Grandmother Models for Contemporary Native Education Pedagogy." In Marie Battiste and Jean Barman, eds., *First Nations Education in Canada: The Circle Unfolds*, pp. 113–123. Vancouver: UBC Press.

Swisher, Karen, and Donna Deyhle. (1989). "The Styles of Learning are Different but the Teaching Just the Same: Suggestions for Teachers of American Indian Youth." *Journal of American Indian Education*. Special issue: pp. 1–14.

Verral, Catherine. (1988). *All My Relations*. Toronto: Canadian Alliance in Solidarity with Native Peoples.

York, Geoffrey. (1989). *The Dispossessed: Life and Death in Native Canada*. London: Vintage U.K.

Appendix 1: Wesakaychak and Wetiko (Told Orally)

Wesakaychak was walking through the world as he always did. One day he approached a village where he saw a teepee, from which small lights flashed. Being very curious, Wesakaychak stopped a man passing by and asked, "What iṣ happening in that teepee?"

"Oh, that is a medicine man's tent, and he is able to tell people their future," the man answered.

"I want to learn my future," thought Wesakaychak, "I think I'll go and see that medicine man."

Wesakaychak got some tobacco and went over to the medicine man's teepee. He gave him the tobacco and was told that he was going to meet Wetiko. Wetiko is a strong and powerful being and it is not known what he is exactly. He is able to yell so loudly that it paralyzes all who hear him. Then he likes to eat his victim. Wesakaychak was warned not to go in heavily wooded places, for there he may come to meet Wetiko.

Wesakaychak continued on his way, walking as best he could in the clearings. He thought a great deal about what the medicine man had said. As he walked, his head bent in thought, he wandered into the forest, and before he knew it, Wetiko appeared before him.

Wesakaychak was frozen with fear. His teeth chattered, and he felt a cold shiver run through his body.

Wetiko shook Wesakaychak and said, "Come on, Wesakaychak, collect some firewood for me. I am very hungry."

Wesakaychak saw that Wetiko meant to eat him, but he saw no way of escaping. He must do what he was told and hope for some chance to change his luck. Perhaps Wetiko would become tired waiting for Wesakaychak to gather wood and make the fire. Perhaps he would fall asleep!

As he worked, Wesakaychak saw an ermine pass him in the forest. "Oh, little brother," said Wesakaychak, "Come here quickly, for I need your help."

Now the ermine was wise about Wesakaychak and his ways. He knew, as did other animals in the world, that Wesakaychak always had some sly

Reprinted from *Nehiyaw Atayoka-we-na: Stories Wesakechak (Cree Legends)* (Saskatoon, Saskatchewan: Curriculum Studies and Research Department, Saskatchewan Indian Cultural College, Federation of Saskatchewan Indians, 1977)

reason for asking their help.

"What do you want of me, Wesakaychak? What sort of trick do you have in mind?" asked the ermine cautiously.

"Little brother, you must help me. Wetiko has captured me and wants to eat me. Please help me! I have a plan, but you must assist me," Wesakaychak pleaded. "When Wetiko opens his mouth, jump down his throat. There you will find a large, beating object. That is his heart. Tear it out with your teeth, and if you do this for me, I will make you the most beautiful of all creatures."

After listening to all this, the ermine took pity on Wesakaychak and decided to help him. After all, Wesakaychak had promised to reward him.

They returned to the place where Wetiko was waiting and found that he had fallen asleep. He lay with his mouth open in a loud snore. The ermine jumped down his throat and Wetiko woke up.

"Wesakaychak, I'm very happy to see you. I am so hungry my heart is hurting me," he cried.

Wesakaychak began to run away, afraid that the ermine had not done his job. Wetiko started up after him and had almost reached Wesakaychak when sharp pain jabbed in his chest. Wetiko fell down. His heart had been torn out and he died on the spot.

The ermine crawled out of Wetiko's mouth. Wesakaychak took the animal tenderly in his arms and washed him. Then he took some clay and began to paint the ermine's body. He painted black around the ermine's eyes and on the tip of his tail. It was a magnificent addition to his red-brown summer coat. But what was even better, in winter he was truly most beautiful, with a snow-white coat, darkened eyes and black-tipped tail.

APPENDIX 2: WESAKAYCHAK AND THE KILLDEER (READ)

Wesakaychak was wandering aimlessly one summer day, for he was bored with himself and his surroundings. Suddenly, he noticed a strange sight. Some killdeer were engaged in a sort of ceremony. He saw them take their eyes out, throw them high up in the air above the willows, and then catch them back into the sockets.

He thought it was an interesting trick to do, and so he approached the birds and said, "My little brothers, teach me how to do that, too."

"No!" replied one bird in a stern voice. "This is a sacred ritual which can only be performed to cure a headache. You can only do this four times a year and no more."

Wesakaychak walked away and wished the killdeer had not spoken so sharply to him.

He had no sooner gotten out of sight, when he slipped back to where he had first seen the birds. Then he changed himself into an old man and painted his face with vermillion. He took a stick in his hand, and, moaning and groaning, walked past the bird, who was still performing the rite.

"What is the matter, old man?" asked the bird.

"Oh, I'm in a miserable state and I don't want to bother you with my problem, because I'll only make you depressed. You see, I have these terrible headaches. My head feels as if it will split." He began to walk slowly by.

"Wait!" said the bird. "Maybe I can help you. Take out your eyes and throw them up to the top of these willows, and don't be afraid because they'll fall back into place again. Always remember not to abuse this gift and don't do it unless it's absolutely necessary. Remember this can be done only four times a year. If you use this gift wisely, it can help you."

Wesakaychak groaned pitifully as he took his eyes out and threw them up in the air. They fell back into place. He was really pleased with himself, for he hadn't ever thought such a thing was possible. He walked away swiftly after assuring the killdeer that the performance had cured him entirely of his headache.

He held his head and began to groan the first time he saw a bunch of

Reprinted from *Nehiyaw Atayoka-we-na: Stories Wesakechak (Cree Legends)* (Saskatoon, Saskatchewan: Curriculum Studies and Research Department, Saskatchewan Indian Cultural College, Federation of Saskatchewan Indians, 1977)

willows. As soon as he came to the willows, he threw his eyes up and then they fell in again. He did this again, then stopped groaning and was on his way again. It was a pleasant way of passing time. He kept pretending to have a headache every time he saw willow trees till he had done it four times, the number of times he was allowed.

However, he wasn't serious about such a sacred rite, and, as everyone knows, this is a dangerous practice. Some misfortune usually befalls one who abuses a sacred rite.

He had not gone much farther when he again pretended to have a headache. He threw his eyes up in the air but much too high. The next thing he knew, they had dropped on the ground instead of falling back into their sockets. He groped around trying to find them, but couldn't. Wesakaychak was blind! Every now and then a stick would prick Wesakaychak in the sockets of his eyes and it was very painful.

Wesakaychak heard a fox laugh at him. No animal had pity for him after all the tricks he had played on them. So, it was the fox who was hurting him! He offered to make the fox's fur beautiful if he would help him, but the fox just laughed and ran away.

Wesakaychak had to do something! He began to walk slowly but kept bumping into trees. Each time he would ask, "What kind of a tree are you?"

"Oh, I am a Birch," would be the reply, or "I am a Poplar."

None of these answers satisfied him. At last, he came upon another tree.

"What kind are you?" he asked.

The tree replied, "I am a Spruce!"

"Oh, the right one!" cried Wesakaychak.

He then collected some dry gum and chewed it till it was soft and pliable. He shaped it to resemble an eye and inserted it into the socket. He then made the other eye. Now he would make the fox pay for his foolish behaviour!

As he was walking along, he came across the fox sleeping on the ground. "Aha!" thought Wesakaychak, "Now is my chance!"

He set a fire around the fox and the fox woke up to find he was trapped. He quickly jumped up and leaped over, trying to escape the flames, but he singed his fur. This is why the red fox is the colour he is today.

APPENDIX 3: QUESTIONS

WESAKAYCHAK AND WETIKO

1. Who are the main characters in this legend?
2. What did Wesakaychak give the medicine man so that he could learn about his future?
3. What are three things you learned about Wetiko from this story?
4. Why was Wetiko glad to see Wesakaychak?
5. What did Wesakaychak promise to give Ermine for helping him?
6. What did Ermine have to do for his special gift?
7. What happened to Wetiko?
8. Describe Ermine after Wesakaychak gave him his gift.

WESAKAYCHAK AND THE KILLDEER

1. Who are the main characters in this legend?
2. Why didn't the killdeer want to teach Wesakaychak the trick of curing headaches?
3. How many times a year could the headache ritual be performed?
4. How did Wesakaychak trick the killdeer into showing him the ritual?
5. Describe the headache ritual.
6. What happened when Wesakaychak performed the ritual the fifth time?
7. Why did the animals have no pity for Wesakaychak?
8. Which tree was Wesakaychak looking for?

APPENDIX 4: DATA ANALYSIS

S#*	Wesakaychak and Witiko Questions								Wesakaychak and the Killdeer Questions							
	1	2	3	4	5	6	7	8	1	2	3	4	5	6	7	8
1	✔	✔	✔	✔	✔	✔	✔		✔							
2	✔	✔	✔	✔	✔		✔	✔	✔			✔		✔		
3	✔	✔	✔	✔	✔	✔	✔	✔	✔		✔					
4	✔	✔	✔	✔	✔	✔	✔	✔								
5	✔		✔	✔	✔	✔	✔	✔								
6	✔		✔	✔	✔	✔	✔	✔	✔		✔		✔	✔		
7	✔	✔	✔	✔	✔	✔	✔	✔	✔		✔	✔		✔		
8	✔	✔	✔	✔	✔	✔	✔	✔	✔		✔		✔	✔		
9	✔		✔		✔	✔	✔		✔							
10	✔	✔		✔	✔	✔	✔		✔							
11	✔	✔		✔		✔	✔	✔	✔							
12	✔		✔	✔	✔				✔		✔					
13	✔		✔	✔	✔	✔	✔	✔	✔		✔			✔	✔	
14	✔	✔	✔	✔	✔	✔	✔	✔	✔		✔	✔	✔	✔	✔	✔
15	✔		✔	✔	✔	✔			✔		✔	✔	✔	✔	✔	✔
16	✔		✔	✔	✔	✔	✔	✔	✔		✔	✔	✔	✔	✔	✔
17	✔	✔	✔	✔	✔	✔	✔	✔	(absent)							

✔ indicates correct answer.

S# indicates student number

Contributors

DR. LILLIAN DYCK is Cree from the Gordon's Reserve; she is also of Asian ancestry. Her father, Yok Leen Quan, was a cook and her mother, the late Eva McNab, was the sister of the late Senator Hilliard McNab from the Gordon's Reserve. Lillian is a full professor without term in the Neuropsychiatry Research Unit, which is part of the Department of Psychiatry at the University of Saskatchewan. She is the mother of one son, Nathan, who is a fourth-year Agricultural and Bioresource Engineering student at the University of Saskatchewan. Lillian is accomplished in many areas and has served as a leader internationally in the areas of women and science. She is a neuroscientist, a feminist, an Aboriginal scholar and brings much strength and dignity to all disciplines. She has published extensively in a number of areas as well. Lillian's efforts over the years were acknowledged during International Women's Week in March 1997 by a citation in the House of Commons for being a role model for girls and women in science. She has done research on how the brain uses chemical transmitters and how drugs, particularly antidepressants, affect neurotransmission. She has also investigated alcohol metabolism in humans and most recently has been studying the bio-distribution and metabolism of new aliphatic propargylamine drugs, which hold promise of being neuronal rescue drugs.

WILLIE ERMINE is Cree and a member of the Sturgeon Lake First Nation. He is program coordinator and lecturer at the Saskatchewan Indian Federated College and a graduate student at the University of Saskatchewan. He resides at Sturgeon Lake with his family, where he maintains contact with his community and is grounded in his culture. He does art work in his spare time and has a great love for the outdoors, where he gets much inspiration for his thoughts. He has published an article, "Aboriginal Epistemology," which speaks of a community perspective in Indigenous knowing and how the community and culture present themselves as grounding for the production of intellect and knowledge. Willie continues to do research into his own people and community for his understanding and has used his findings to critically look at Western systems of knowing and to enhance his students' understanding of traditional Cree knowledge.

JANE HARP née McCALLUM is Cree and a single mother of two beautiful children, a 29-year-old son and a 19-year-old daughter. Jane is a survivor of the residential era that weakened and in some cases fragmented and devastated the Aboriginal family unit. Even so, her Cree language and Native pride are still intact. Jane is a social worker and has worked for various Native organizations in Manitoba and Saskatchewan. She holds a B.A. from the University of Winnipeg and a Bachelor of Social Work from the University of Manitoba. She just completed her Master's in Social Work at Carleton University, Ottawa.

BENTE HUNTLEY is a Cree Metis from the Muskoday First Nation. Currently she works at the Saskatchewan Urban Native Teacher Education Centre (SUNTEP) in Prince Albert, Saskatchewan, teaching English 99 and the science methods class. She grew up in a rural community east of Prince Albert, where she spent summers with her grandparents on Muskoday Reserve. These were her first teachers who instilled the fascinating world of plants and survival. Science has been a lifelong interest for her. Currently, she is completing a Master's degree at the Department of Curriculum Studies, College of Education, University of Saskatchewan. Because of her background and interest in the natural sciences, she chose to research the traditional knowledge of Canada's original inhabitants.

WALLY ISBISTER is from the Ahtahkakoop Reserve, home of Chief John Starblanket, one of the head chiefs who signed Treaty 6 at Carleton. Wally credits his academic success and athletic accomplishments to his rich heritage, supportive family and great support from his band. His mother and father encouraged him; his brothers and sisters supported him; his wife stood beside him through "thick and thin"; and his two sons blessed him with six grandchildren. He brings thirty-six years of experience to education. At the time of writing his essay, he was enrolled in a post-graduate program with the Indian and Northern Education Program, Department of Educational Foundations, University of Saskatchewan. He is now involved in the bicultural aspects of education.

MARYANNE LANIGAN is Irish-Metis, was born in Big River, Saskatchewan, is the mother of two children and has been a teacher with Saskatoon Catholic schools for seventeen years. Mary Anne received her B.Ed. and her B.A. (Honours) in Native Studies from the University of Saskatchewan. Her current research interests include storytelling and the Grey Nun schools in northern Saskatchewan. Presently, she serves as Executive Member of the Saskatchewan Teachers Association and as System Coordinator for Catholic Schools.

DR. LENORE A. STIFFARM is an enrolled Ahahninin from the Fort Belknap Reserve, Montana, with Nakota and Kainai ancestry. She is the mother to three beautiful human beings: White Moon, They-Wus and Medicine Eagle. Lenore currently serves as Associate Professor, Indian and Northern Education Program, Department of Educational Foundations, College of Education, University of Saskatchewan. Her undergraduate work in education was at the University of Montana, Missoula, Montana, and she received three degrees from Harvard University: an M.Ed. in 1976; a Certificate of Advanced Study, 1977; and a doctorate in Education, 1980. Her doctoral requirements were fulfilled in the area of "Managing Change in Boston School System: An Examination of Criteria for School Closings in Boston, September 1978–December 1979." Her research and publishing interests include demography, discrimination and inequality, racism, healing and wellness, curriculum development, Aboriginal parenting, and spirit writing. She is currently researching how Aboriginal women experience and respond to racism using their own ways of knowing and ways of being.

IDA SWAN is a Cree born in Sandy Narrows, Saskatchewan. She attended elementary school in Pelican Narros, spent three years in a residential school, received a high school diploma, and then earned a teaching certificate in 1970, a B.Ed. from the University of Saskatchewan in 1986 and a post-graduate diploma in Educational Foundations in 1998. Her current interests are in the decolonization of the school curriculum and the preservation of the Cree language. She and her husband Edward have four children.

ANGELINA WEENIE is a Cree Indian from Sweetgrass Reserve, Saskatchewan. She is presently a lecturer at the Saskatchewan Indian Federated College, Regina campus. She has a B.Ed. and B.A. degrees from the University of Saskatchewan, and a post-graduate diploma from the Indian and Northern Education Program, Department of Educational Foundations, University of Saskatchewan. Her research interests include exploring First Nations language methodologies.

GLOSSARY

Ethos: The characteristic habits and attitudes of the totality that contributes and creates the spirit of the home community.

Medicine Wheel: This is a Plains Indian model of the sacred circle, which shows interconnectedness and is cyclical. The four dimensions of East, South, West and North correspond to the four potentialities of Spiritual, Emotional, Physical and Mental.

Modelling: This process is reality-oriented and involves every aspect of Aboriginal culture. It is the means of understanding anything and everything on Earth that affects the people. It creates a sense of connectedness with the physical, mental, psychological and spiritual world of the Northern Cree.

Myths: These are the sacred truths of people. Strict protocol must be followed when telling myths. Only a prescribed storyteller should tell the sacred myths. These myths are to be told only during the winter. It is important that the myths be told accurately, so a training or apprenticeship is required. Each myth has more than one meaning.

Narratives: Narratives provide an oral account of the historical events of First Nations. These narratives were committed to memory. There were also personal narratives of families and their deeds. Narratives give pride and confidence to the young.

Protocol: "[A]ny one of a number of culturally ordained actions and statements, established by ancient tradition, that an individual completes to establish a relationship with another person from whom the individual makes a request." (Walter Lightning, "Compassionate Mind: Implications of a Text Written by Elder Louis Sunchild," *Canadian Journal of Native Education* 19, p. 216.)

Smudge: This is how we purify ourselves before an important ceremony, releasing any energy we want to let go of so that we can be totally present for the ceremony we are about to enter. Sage is one of the plants that groups on the prairies use. We rub a ball of sage on our bodies, symbolically removing any energy. We pick this sage each year in June and July. Smudging also occurs in the form of lighting sage, cedar and/or sweet grass. For certain ceremonies, select "medicines" are used. However, there is a protocol within various First Nations about who can smudge as well as when women can smudge, depending on the time of the month and time in life. There is also a specific protocol as to how and when one enters the circle to smudge.

Spirit Writing: A process whereby one writes from the spirit and does not worry about dotting the *i*'s and crossing the *t*'s. One writes about whatever comes as a process of washing and healing one's spirit.

Storytelling: Storytelling is the oldest form of the arts. It is the basis of all other arts—drama, art, dance and music. It has been and is an important part of every culture. It is necessary for the revitalization of First Nations cultures and can be a starting point for moving away from assimilationist to liberationist education. This process combines both myth and narrative.

Traditional Environmental Knowledge: The nature of Aboriginal epistemology—how Aboriginal peoples attain their knowledge of the environment.

Writing Circles: Aboriginal culture and ceremony are the foundation for these circles. Aboriginal music is used and "smudge" is incorporated into the healing process. Where possible, the burning of the writing produced in this process is done to symbolize letting go of anything one is holding within. These circles are often mistakenly considered a language arts writing experience. They are safe places where Aboriginal peoples are allowed to heal together.